SOLITARY WITCHCRAFT

A MODERN GUIDE TO WALKING THE WITCH'S PATH ALONE

ANCIENT MAGICK FOR TODAY'S WITCH SERIES
BOOK 15

MONIQUE JOINER SIEDLAK

OSHUN
PUBLICATIONS
oshunpublications.com

Ancient Magick for
Today's Witch Series

SOLITARY WITCHCRAFT

A Modern Guide to Walking the
Witch's Path Alone

MONIQUE JOINER SIEDLAK

OSHUN
PUBLICATIONS
oshunpublications.com

Cover Design by MJS

Cover Image by Midjourney

Published by Oshun Publications

www.oshunpublications.com

ANCIENT MAGICK FOR TODAY'S WITCH SERIES

The *Ancient Magick for Today's Witch Series* is a series for modern witches to explore ancient magick, covering Celtic, Gypsy, and Crystal magic, among others. It offers practical advice on spells, rituals, and enchantments for today's use, incorporating natural energies and spiritual connections. With insights into Shamanism, Wicca, and more, it helps readers enhance their magickal journey, offering paths to protection, prosperity, and spiritual growth by combining ancient wisdom with contemporary practice.

Wiccan Basics

Candle Magick

Wiccan Spells

Love Spells

Abundance Spells

Herb Magick

Moon Magick

AVAILABLE IN AUDIO

MOON MAGICK

MONIQUE JOINER SIEDLAK

MOJOSIEDLAK.COM/AUDIOBOOKS

CONTENTS

INTRODUCTION TO SOLITARY WITCHCRAFT

Solitary witchcraft represents not just a path but a personal journey within the expansive realms of witchcraft and spirituality. It diverges from the traditional, communal practices found within covens, steering instead towards a solitary exploration of the mystical, the magical, and the self. This unique form of witchcraft empowers individuals to forge their own connections with the elements, the divine, and the profound depths of their inner worlds, free from the confines of structured group rituals and teachings.

At its essence, solitary witchcraft is a manifestation of spiritual autonomy. It offers a flexible framework within which practitioners can explore various facets of witchcraft, including spellcraft, divination, herbalism, and the veneration of deities, all tailored to their personal beliefs, interests, and rhythms. This path appeals to those who seek a personal and direct relationship with the natural and spiritual worlds, often leading to an individualized practice that evolves over time.

The significance of solitary witchcraft in the modern spiritual landscape cannot be overstated. It stands as a testament to the enduring human desire for connection, understanding, and empowerment through the ancient arts of magic and witchcraft. In a world where organized religion and communal spiritual practices dominate, solitary witchcraft offers an alternative route to spiritual fulfillment, one that emphasizes personal intuition, self-guided learning, and the freedom to explore the vastness of the unseen world at one's own pace.

This chapter aims to shed light on the nuances of solitary witchcraft, tracing its historical roots, examining its modern adaptations, and exploring the benefits and challenges of walking the solitary path. Through this exploration, readers will gain insight into the diverse and personal practice of solitary witchcraft, understanding its role not just in the history of spirituality but in the lives of contemporary practitioners seeking empowerment and personal growth through the ancient craft.

As we delve into the world of solitary witchcraft, we invite you to open your mind to the possibilities that lie within the realm of personal spiritual practice. Whether you are a seasoned practitioner or new to the path, this introduction serves as a gateway to the transformative power of solitary witchcraft, offering a foundation upon which to build a practice that resonates with your innermost self.

Understanding Solitary Witchcraft

Solitary witchcraft, at its core, is the practice of witchcraft conducted alone, without the formal structure or support of a coven or group. This path is chosen by those who feel called to explore their spiritual journey in a personal and individualized way. It is defined by a sense of autonomy, allowing practitioners to delve into their craft according to their own rules, intuition, and connection with the natural and spiritual worlds.

Key Characteristics

The key characteristics of solitary witchcraft include a strong emphasis on personal intuition, self-guided learning, and the freedom to draw from a variety of sources and traditions. Solitary witches often curate their practice by combining elements from different paths that resonate with them, whether those elements are rituals, deities, spells, or philosophies. This eclectic approach is not about cherry-picking superficially but about forming a coherent, personal spiritual practice that aligns with one's own beliefs and values.

Unlike coven-based witchcraft, where rituals and practices are often decided collectively and guided by more experienced practitioners, solitary witchcraft is marked by self-discovery and self-teaching. Books, the internet, and one's own experiences become the teachers. The practice is fluid, evolving with the practitioner's own spiritual journey and life circumstances.

Comparison with Coven-Based Practices

While coven-based witchcraft offers community, shared rituals, and mentorship, it also comes with structured teachings and a degree of hierarchy. In contrast, solitary witchcraft is democratized and self-directed, offering unparalleled freedom but also requiring a higher degree of self-motivation and discipline. The solitary path allows for a personal exploration of witchcraft at one's own pace and according to one's own changing needs and insights.

One of the most significant differences is the solitary witch's ability to integrate their practice seamlessly into daily life, making their entire life a sacred practice. This integration speaks to the personal and immersive nature of solitary witchcraft, where the boundary between the mundane and the magical is blurred, allowing for a constant dialogue with the divine in all aspects of life.

The Solitary Witch's Path: A Journey of Self-Discovery and Empowerment

The path of a solitary witch is a journey of self-discovery and empowerment. It is about taking personal responsibility for one's spiritual growth and finding strength and wisdom within oneself. This path challenges practitioners to listen to their inner voices and to connect with the natural world and the energies that surround them in a direct, unmediated way.

The journey is as much about self-awareness and personal development as it is about practicing witchcraft. Solitary witches often find that their practice becomes a tool for personal transformation, helping them to understand themselves better, to heal, and to manifest their true desires and intentions in the world.

Despite the solitary nature of the path, many witches find a sense of connection and community through shared experiences. This connection underscores the fact that while the practice itself is solitary, the journey is shared with countless others walking similar paths.

Solitary witchcraft is a path of freedom, personal responsibility, and deep spiritual engagement. It offers a unique way to explore the mysteries of life and the universe, guided by one's own inner light and the vast tapestry of witchcraft traditions from around the world. For those drawn to this solitary journey, it opens the door to a profound and transformative personal practice, where the discovery of one's true self and the exploration of the unseen realms go hand in hand.

Historical Context of Solitary Witchcraft

The roots of solitary witchcraft stretch back to the dawn of human spirituality, intertwined with the earliest practices of magic and communion with the natural world. While the term "witchcraft" itself carries a complex and varied history, elements of what we now recognize as solitary witchcraft have been present across cultures and epochs, often manifesting as individual acts of magic, healing, and divination.

Early Mentions and Practices

In ancient times, the figure of the wise woman, the herbalist, or the shaman often practiced what could be considered a form of solitary witchcraft. These individuals served their communities through their knowledge of the natural world, healing arts, and their connection to the spiritual realms. They were the custodians of their communities' spiritual well-being, working often in solitude to mediate between the worlds of the human and the divine.

The practices and beliefs of these early practitioners were rooted in their local environments and cultures, forming an organic and intuitive relationship with the land and its spirits. This intimate connection with nature is a hallmark of solitary witchcraft, reflecting a universal human experience of seeking understanding and power within the natural world.

Evolution from Ancient Times to the Middle Ages

As societies evolved and became more complex, the role of the solitary practitioner also transformed. The spread of monotheistic religions and the institutionalization of spiritual practices often marginalized or demonized these solitary figures. The Middle Ages in Europe, in particular, saw a drastic shift in the perception of witchcraft, with the solitary witch often becoming vilified as an evil figure in league with demonic forces.

However, despite persecution, the practices and knowledge of solitary witchcraft persisted, often in secret. The survival of these traditions can be attributed to the flexibility and adaptability of solitary practitioners, who were able to keep their practices alive by weaving them into the fabric of folk customs and lore.

The Renaissance to Modern Times: The Revival and Transformation

The Renaissance period, with its renewed interest in the occult and the mysteries of the natural world, provided a fertile ground for the revival of witchcraft practices, including solitary witchcraft. This revival was not without its challenges, as witch hunts and persecution continued well into the modern era in some parts of the world.

However, the 20th century saw a significant turning point with the emergence of the New Age movement and the rekindling of interest in pagan and nature-based spirituality. The publication of seminal works on witchcraft and magic, along with the increasing availability of historical and anthropological research, allowed for a broader understanding and acceptance of solitary witchcraft.

Modern Revival

The modern revival of solitary witchcraft has been characterized by the reclamation of the term "witchcraft" as a positive and empowering practice. Solitary witches today draw from a rich tapestry of historical and cultural traditions while also incorporating contemporary beliefs and values. This modern adaptation emphasizes personal empowerment, ecological awareness, and the development of a personal spiritual practice that respects the diversity of the witchcraft tradition.

The historical context of solitary witchcraft underscores its resilience and adaptability. From the wise women and shamans of ancient times to the solitary practitioners of today, the path of solitary witchcraft has evolved while retaining its core essence: a personal connection to the natural and spiritual worlds. This historical journey highlights the enduring human desire for knowledge, power, and connection and the role of solitary witchcraft in fulfilling these timeless pursuits.

1

MODERN ADAPTATION OF SOLITARY WITCHCRAFT

The landscape of solitary witchcraft has undergone profound changes in the modern era, evolving in response to technological advancements, shifts in societal values, and the expanding accessibility of information. Today, solitary witchcraft reflects a blend of ancient traditions and contemporary practices, embodying the flexibility and resilience that have always been at its core.

Impact of Technology and the Internet

One of the most significant catalysts for the modern adaptation of solitary witchcraft has been the advent of technology, particularly the internet. Digital platforms have revolutionized how solitary witches connect, learn, and share their practices. Online forums, social media groups, and digital libraries offer an unprecedented wealth of resources, allowing practitioners to access a wide range of materials, from ancient texts to contemporary guides on witchcraft, at the click of a button.

The internet has also facilitated the formation of virtual communities, providing solitary practitioners with a sense of belonging and an opportunity to share experiences, knowledge, and support with like-minded individuals from around the globe. This virtual connectivity has been especially valuable for those who, due to geographic isolation or social stigma, might otherwise struggle to find community and resources.

Role of Books, Online Communities, and Virtual Covens

While technology has opened new avenues for learning and connection, traditional resources like books continue to play a crucial role in the practice of solitary witchcraft. The works of pioneering authors and scholars have laid the foundations for modern witchcraft practices, offering insights into rituals, spells, and philosophical underpinnings of various witchcraft traditions. These texts, alongside online resources, serve as vital tools for education and inspiration, enabling solitary witches to craft their unique path.

Online communities and virtual covens have emerged as spaces for collaboration, learning, and ritual practice that transcend physical boundaries. These platforms offer workshops, guided rituals, and discussions, enriching the solitary practitioner's experience by providing a sense of communal engagement without compromising their autonomy.

Integration of Modern Beliefs and Values

Contemporary solitary witchcraft is characterized by an inclusive and eclectic approach, integrating modern beliefs and values such as environmentalism, feminism, and social justice. Many solitary witches view their practice as not only a spiritual path but also a means to effect positive change, both personally and globally. This integration reflects a broader shift towards a spirituality that is rooted in the realities of the modern world, advocating for healing, empowerment, and transformation on both an individual and collective level.

The adaptation of solitary witchcraft in the modern era underscores its dynamic nature, highlighting how traditional practices can evolve to meet the needs and challenges of the contemporary world. By embracing technology, fostering online communities, and integrating contemporary values, solitary witchcraft continues to offer a rich and empowering path for those seeking a personal connection with the spiritual and natural worlds.

Benefits of Practicing Alone

Solitary witchcraft, with its emphasis on personal autonomy and flexibility, offers a range of benefits that cater to the individual's spiritual growth and self-discovery. This path allows practitioners to tailor their practice to their unique needs, beliefs, and circumstances, fostering a personal connection to their spirituality.

Personal Freedom and Flexibility

One of the most significant benefits of practicing solitary witchcraft is the unparalleled personal freedom it offers. Without the need to conform to group schedules, hierarchies, or specific traditions, solitary witches can explore various aspects of witchcraft at their own pace and on their own terms. This flexibility enables practitioners to integrate their craft into their daily lives seamlessly, allowing for a living practice that evolves with their personal growth and life changes.

Deepened Self-Awareness and Spiritual Connection

Solitary witchcraft encourages a journey inward, prompting practitioners to engage in self-reflection and meditation as they explore their path. This reflective practice fosters deepened self-awareness, enabling witches to understand their strengths, weaknesses, desires, and fears more. Moreover, the solitary path offers a unique opportunity to develop a personal connection with the divine, the natural world, and the unseen forces that shape our existence. This direct and personal relationship with spirituality can be immensely fulfilling, offering guidance, comfort, and empowerment.

Creativity and Personalization of Rituals

Without the constraints of group practices, solitary witches have the creative freedom to design and personalize their rituals, spells, and ceremonies. This aspect of solitary witchcraft not only enhances the personal relevance and effectiveness of these practices but also encourages creative exploration of the self and the craft. The ability to adapt rituals to reflect personal beliefs, goals, and current circumstances makes the practice of solitary witchcraft a dynamic and evolving journey of spiritual expression.

Enhanced Learning and Growth

The path of solitary witchcraft is one of continual learning and growth. The responsibility to seek out knowledge, discern truth from misinformation, and develop a coherent practice challenges solitary witches to become proactive learners. This self-directed learning process encourages a broad exploration of witchcraft, including its history, philosophies, and various traditions, leading to a well-rounded and informed practice. The growth that comes from navigating the vast landscape of witchcraft alone is both a challenge and a reward, offering a profound sense of achievement and personal empowerment.

Practicing solitary witchcraft brings with it a wealth of opportunities for personal transformation, spiritual exploration, and creative expression. The benefits of this path lie not only in the freedom and flexibility it offers but also in the deep personal fulfillment and empowerment that come from walking a self-directed spiritual journey.

Challenges of Solitary Witchcraft

While the solitary path offers unique benefits, it also presents specific challenges that can test practitioners' resolve and dedication. Navigating these challenges is a crucial part of the journey, fostering resilience and a deeper commitment to the craft.

Lack of Community Support and Mentorship

One of the most significant challenges faced by solitary witches is the absence of a physical community and the mentorship that can come from more experienced practitioners. The guidance, support, and shared wisdom of a community or coven can be invaluable, especially for beginners. Solitary practitioners must often rely on their own resources to learn and grow, which can be daunting and, at times, isolating.

Overcoming this challenge involves:

- Seeking out virtual communities.
- Engaging with online forums.
- Participating in social media groups dedicated to witchcraft.

These platforms can offer a sense of belonging and provide access to a wealth of shared knowledge and experiences. Additionally, books, workshops, and online courses can serve as surrogate mentors, guiding solitary witches on their path.

The Struggle with Self-Discipline and Motivation

Practicing witchcraft alone requires significant self-discipline and motivation. Without the structure of group rituals or the accountability that comes with belonging to a coven, maintaining a consistent practice can be challenging. The solitary path demands that practitioners set their own goals, schedule their practices, and find the motivation to continue learning and growing independently.

To address this challenge, solitary witches can set clear, achievable goals for their practice and establish regular rituals or milestones. Creating a dedicated sacred space for practice can also help in establishing a routine. Keeping a journal or a book of shadows to track progress, experiences, and reflections can serve as a motivational tool and a personal testament to the journey's evolution.

Finding Reliable Resources and Avoiding Misinformation

In an age of abundant and easily accessible information, discerning reliable resources from misinformation can be overwhelming. The solitary witch must navigate a vast landscape of books, websites, and social media content, making critical judgments about the accuracy and integrity of the information encountered.

Cultivating critical thinking skills and cross-referencing sources can help in evaluating the reliability of information. Seeking out well-reviewed and recommended resources, as well as engaging with established and respected communities, can guide practitioners toward trustworthy details. Additionally, listening to one's intuition can be a valuable tool in discerning the quality and relevance of the material.

Despite these challenges, the solitary path remains a rewarding and transformative journey for those who choose to walk it. The obstacles encountered along the way can serve as opportunities for growth, fostering a practice that is resilient, flexible, and personal. By confronting these challenges with determination and an open heart, solitary witches can deepen their practice and strengthen their connection to the craft.

2

CREATING YOUR SACRED SPACE

In the realm of personal spirituality and witchcraft, the creation of a sacred space is a profound step toward deepening one's connection to the universe, the divine, and the self. Defined broadly, a sacred space is an area set aside for rituals, meditation, and spiritual practices. In this physical and symbolic haven, the mundane world can be transcended. This concept, found across myriad spiritual traditions, underpins the human desire for connection with something greater than oneself. Whether it's a corner of a room adorned with personal totems and symbols or a quiet spot in a forest where one feels the whisper of the divine, a sacred space is where the spiritual journey is nurtured and celebrated. This chapter aims to guide you through the process of creating, maintaining, and utilizing a sacred space that resonates with your unique spiritual path, enhancing your practices of witchcraft, meditation, or contemplation.

Understanding Sacred Spaces

Sacred spaces have been integral to spiritual practices and rituals across cultures and epochs, serving as tangible connections to the divine, the natural world, and the inner self. These spaces, dedicated to meditation, reflection, and the practice of witchcraft, are as diverse as the traditions from which they emerge. Their historical and cultural significance is profound, offering insights into human spirituality and our innate desire to connect with something greater than ourselves.

Historical and Cultural Context

Throughout history, sacred spaces have manifested in myriad forms, from the natural sanctuaries of ancient forests and stone circles to the constructed sanctity of temples, churches, and home altars. These spaces have played pivotal roles in spiritual practices, acting as gateways to other realms and focal points for gathering spiritual energy in ancient civilizations, such as Egypt and Mesopotamia, temples not only served as places of worship but also as cosmic axes that connected the heavens and the earth, embodying the intersection of the divine and the mundane.

In indigenous cultures around the world, nature itself has often been revered as a sacred space, with mountains, rivers, and forests seen as embodiments of spirits or gods. These beliefs highlight the universal human recognition of particular places as being imbued with spiritual significance, power, and presence.

Psychological and Spiritual Benefits

The creation of a personal sacred space in contemporary practice draws on this rich history, offering significant psychological and spiritual benefits. Psychologically, having a dedicated space for spiritual activities can foster focus, tranquility, and a sense of sanctuary from the everyday world. It creates a physical boundary that, when crossed, signals a shift from mundane to sacred, aiding in the transition to a meditative or ritual mindset.

Spiritually, a sacred space acts as a personal conduit for connecting with the divine or the practitioner's higher self. It becomes a vessel for spiritual energy, facilitating more in-depth meditation, more potent rituals, and a heightened sense of presence and connection. This space can become a personal microcosm, reflecting the universe's macrocosm and the practitioner's place within it.

Variations of Sacred Spaces

Sacred spaces can vary significantly in form and function, reflecting the individual's spiritual path and circumstances. An altar, for example, might be adorned with symbols of the divine, candles, crystals, and tools for ritual work, serving as a focus for spellcasting or worship. For others, a sacred space might be a minimalist corner dedicated to meditation, with little more than a cushion and a single symbol of personal significance.

Nature itself can also serve as a sacred space. Practices take place in forests, by bodies of water, or under the open sky, connecting the practitioner directly with the natural world's energies.

In shared or limited spaces, portable sacred spaces have become a practical adaptation, with practitioners using boxes or trays that can be set up and taken down as needed. These spaces, though temporary in setup, are no less significant, embodying the same intent and purpose as more permanent installations.

Understanding the depth and diversity of sacred spaces enriches the process of creating one's own. It underscores the idea that the essence of a sacred space lies not in its outward form but in its ability to connect the practitioner to their spiritual path, to the divine, and to the deeper aspects of themselves. Whether through elaborate altars, serene nature spots, or simple, quiet corners, sacred spaces serve as foundational elements of personal spirituality, offering solace, inspiration, and a profound connection to the unseen.

Choosing Your Space

The selection of a sacred space within your personal environment is a critical step in establishing a place of power, reflection, and spiritual practice. This choice, influenced by practical considerations as well as intuitive feeling, should be approached with thoughtfulness and intention. Here's how to navigate the process of choosing the suitable space for your sacred practices, ensuring it aligns with your spiritual needs and the practicalities of your living situation.

Criteria for Selection

The ideal sacred space resonates with you on a personal level, offering a sense of peace, inspiration, and spiritual connectivity. It should be a place where you can comfortably sit or stand, meditate, perform rituals, and engage in whatever practices form the core of your spiritual path.

Consider the following criteria when selecting your space:

Privacy: A space where you can practice without interruption or distraction is ideal. Privacy supports a deeper engagement with your spiritual work, free from the concerns of being observed or disturbed.

Ambiance: Look for a space that naturally invites a sense of calm and serenity. Elements like natural light, a view of nature, or simply a quiet corner of your home can significantly enhance the ambiance.

Energetic Feel: Trust your intuition about the energy of a potential space. Some areas within a home or outdoors naturally feel more conducive to spiritual work. You might be drawn to a particular room or spot because it feels inherently sacred or peaceful.

Considerations for Limited or Shared Spaces

Many practitioners face the challenge of creating a sacred space within a small living area or a home shared with others who might not share their spiritual beliefs.

In such cases, flexibility and creativity become essential tools in establishing your sacred space:

Portability: For those with limited space or the need to keep their practices private, consider creating a portable sacred space. This can be a small altar on a tray or a box that contains your spiritual tools and symbols, which you can set up for use and then store away.

Multipurpose Areas: A part of a room that serves another purpose can also be transformed into a sacred space when needed. For instance, a corner of your bedroom or living room can be designated for spiritual work, using a shelf or a small table as a focal point. This area can be easily integrated into the room's overall function without being permanently set aside.

Natural Spaces: If dedicating an indoor space is particularly challenging, look to nature. Gardens, parks, or even quiet streets with trees can serve as temporary sacred spaces where you can connect with the natural world and conduct your practices.

Making the Choice

Once you've considered the practical aspects of your living situation and the energetic feel of potential spaces, making your choice often comes down to a gut feeling. The right space feels like a sanctuary, even if it's as simple as a chair facing a window where the morning light streams in or a spot on the floor beside your favorite plant.

After selecting your space, spend some time there in quiet contemplation or meditation. This initial period of simply being in the space can help solidify your connection to it and begin the process of infusing it with your personal energy and intention.

Choosing your sacred space is a personal journey that sets the foundation for your spiritual practices. Whether you have an entire room to dedicate or a small corner of a shared space, the key is to approach this choice with intention, respect for your needs, and openness to the possibilities it brings to your spiritual path.

Cleansing and Consecrating Your Space

Creating a sacred space involves more than just selecting a location; it requires energetically preparing the area to align with your spiritual intentions. This process involves two critical steps: cleansing and consecrating. Cleansing removes any negative or stagnant energy present while consecrating the space dedicates it to your spiritual work, inviting in positive energies and setting protective boundaries.

Cleansing Your Space

Cleansing is the first step in transforming a physical area into a sacred space. This act purifies the environment, creating a clean slate for your spiritual practices. Various methods can be employed, each tradition offering its own techniques.

Here are some widely used cleansing methods:

Smoke Cleansing: Burning herbs like sage, lavender, or Palo Santo is a traditional way to cleanse a space. The smoke is believed to carry away negative energies. Light your chosen herb, allowing the smoke to waft through the area. Pay special attention to corners and entryways where stagnant energy may collect.

Sound Cleansing: Sound vibrations from bells, singing bowls, or even clapping can break up stagnant energy. Move through your space, making noise with your chosen instrument, envisioning the vibrations clearing away negativity.

Salt and Water: Salt is known for its purifying properties, and water is often associated with cleansing. Mix sea salt into water and sprinkle it in your space, or use a saltwater spray. This method combines elemental energies to purify your area.

Visualization: For those preferring a non-physical method, visualization can be powerful. Imagine a bright light or a flame moving through your space, burning away negative energies and filling the area with purity and peace.

Consecrating Your Space

Once cleansed, consecrating your space, dedicate it to your spiritual work, setting the intention for its use and inviting protective and positive energies. This step personalizes the space, aligning it with your specific spiritual path and goals. Consecration can be as simple or elaborate as you choose.

Here are some general steps to consider:

Set Your Intentions: Begin by clearly stating your purpose for the space. This can be done aloud or silently, focusing on your spiritual goals and the types of energies you wish to attract.

Invite Protective Energies: Call in any deities, spirits, ancestors, or universal energies you work with, asking for their protection and blessings. This can be done through prayer, chanting, or simply speaking from the heart.

Use Symbols: Place symbols, talismans, or objects of personal significance in your space as physical representations of your intentions. These can be items that correspond to your spiritual path or personal items that hold deep meaning.

Light and Offerings: Lighting a candle or incense can signify the activation of your sacred space, while offerings like flowers, stones, or food can honor the protective energies or deities you've invited.

Maintaining the Sacredness

Regularly cleansing and re-consecrating your space can help maintain its sacredness, especially if it's in a shared area or if you perform intense spiritual work there. This not only reaffirms your intentions but also keeps the energy fresh and aligned with your spiritual journey.

Creating a sacred space is a dynamic process that evolves with your spiritual path. Cleansing and consecrating are foundational practices that transform a mere physical location into a powerful spiritual sanctuary, enhancing your connection to the divine, the natural world, and your inner self. Through these acts of purification and dedication, your sacred space becomes a focal point for deep spiritual work, growth, and transformation.

Decorating and Personalizing Your Space

After cleansing and consecrating your sacred space, the next step is to decorate and personalize it, transforming it into a reflection of your unique spiritual path. This phase is not only about beautification but about infusing the space with items that carry deep personal and spiritual significance.

The decoration process involves:

- Selecting symbols, tools, and artifacts that resonate with your practice.
- Enhancing the energy of the space.
- Aligning it with your intentions.

Selecting Elements for Your Space

When choosing items for your sacred space, consider their symbolic meaning and energetic qualities. Each element should serve a purpose, whether for use in rituals, as a focus for meditation, or as an embodiment of specific energies.

Common elements include:

Altars: Many choose to center their sacred space around an altar, a focal point for spiritual practices. An altar can hold ritual tools, symbols of the elements (earth, air, fire, water), and representations of deities or spiritual guides.

Natural Elements: Incorporating nature into your space can help ground your practices and connect you to the earth's energy. Consider adding crystals, stones, plants, water features, or bowls of salt or soil.

Symbols and Artifacts: Items that represent your spiritual beliefs or personal journey can add depth and meaning to your space. This might include religious symbols, statues, tarot cards, runes, or personal talismans.

Lighting: Candles, lanterns, or fairy lights can create a serene ambiance. The light symbolizes guidance, clarity, and the element of fire. Choosing different colors can align with various intentions or magical purposes.

Textiles: Rugs, cushions, tapestries, or altar cloths in fabrics and colors that resonate with your spiritual practice can add comfort and aesthetic appeal while also defining the space.

Personalization Through Intention

As you decorate your sacred space, do so with intention. Each item you place should feel like a conscious choice, contributing to the space's overall energy and purpose. Personalization makes your sacred space truly yours, a sanctuary tailored to your spiritual needs and aesthetic preferences.

Creating an Altar: If you choose to have an altar, arrange it in a way that feels balanced and harmonious to you. Some follow traditional layouts, placing items to represent the cardinal directions or elements, while others let intuition guide their arrangement.

Seasonal and Personal Changes: Your sacred space can evolve with you. Feel free to adjust its layout, add new items, or remove those that no longer serve your practice. Incorporating seasonal elements can also keep the space energetically aligned with the natural world.

Aesthetic and Energy Balance: While the visual appeal of your sacred space is essential, ensure that the aesthetic choices also align with the energetic qualities you wish to cultivate.

Harmony between the visual and energetic aspects creates a more powerful and cohesive space.

Engaging the Senses

A truly personalized sacred space engages all the senses, creating a multi-dimensional experience that deepens your spiritual practice. Consider incorporating elements that appeal to sight, sound, touch, smell, and even taste through offerings or ritual elements. This sensory richness can enhance your connection to the present moment and the specific energies you're working with.

Decorating and personalizing your sacred space is a rewarding process, allowing you to express your spirituality in tangible forms. Through careful selection and intentional placement of items, you create not just a space for practice but a reflection of your inner world, a haven for growth, and a conduit for the divine.

Maintaining Your Sacred Space

Creating a sacred space is a profound step in one's spiritual journey, but maintaining that space is equally important. A well-maintained sacred space continues to be a source of spiritual nourishment, a place where your energies are uplifted and your practice deepens. Regular care ensures that the space remains vibrant, energetically supportive, and aligned with your intentions. Here's how to keep your sacred space a potent catalyst for your spiritual growth.

Routine Cleansing

Just as you initially cleansed your space to prepare it for spiritual work, regular cleansing helps to clear any stagnant or negative energies that may accumulate over time. This can be especially important after intense emotional periods, significant life changes, or deep spiritual work that might disrupt the energetic balance of the space. Employ the same methods used during the initial cleansing—such as smoke from sage or Palo Santo, sound vibrations, or saltwater spritzing—on a regular basis, depending on your intuition and the frequency of your space's use.

Re-Consecrating the Space

Over time, the specific focus of your spiritual practice may shift. Periodically re-consecrating your sacred space can realign it with your current intentions, goals, and spiritual path. This might involve a simple ritual where you reaffirm your space's purpose, invite protective energies, and perhaps introduce new symbols or elements that reflect your evolving journey. Re-consecration is a powerful way to renew your commitment to your practice and ensure your sacred space remains a true reflection of your spiritual aspirations.

Refreshing Decorations and Tools

As you grow and change, so too will the elements of your sacred space. Regularly evaluate whether the items, decorations, and tools still resonate with your current path. You might find that particular objects no longer hold the same significance, or you may acquire new items that more accurately reflect your spiritual development. Refreshing your space not only keeps it energetically aligned with your practice but also reinvigorates your connection to the area, making it feel alive and dynamic.

Energetic Offerings

Making energetic offerings is another way to maintain the vibrancy of your sacred space. Offerings can be anything that holds personal significance or is considered valuable to the energies or deities you work with. This might include fresh flowers, food items, crystals charged with specific intentions, or simply your gratitude and prayers. Offerings are a way of showing respect and appreciation for the spiritual support you receive. They can significantly enhance the energetic ambiance of your space.

Engaging with Your Space

The most crucial aspect of maintaining your sacred space is to regularly engage with it. Whether through meditation, ritual work, contemplation, or simply sitting in silence, your presence activates the space. Regular use not only charges it with your personal energy but also deepens your connection to the spiritual dimensions your space represents.

Flexibility and Growth

Recognize that maintaining your sacred space is not about keeping it static but allowing it to evolve. Be open to changes that reflect your spiritual growth and the natural cycles of life. This flexibility ensures that your sacred space remains a true sanctuary for your evolving spiritual journey.

Maintaining your sacred space is an ongoing process of engagement, reflection, and care. It's about nurturing a relationship with your practice, the divine, and yourself. Through regular maintenance, your sacred space remains a potent and vibrant cornerstone of your spiritual practice, supporting your journey and reflecting your inner growth.

Utilizing Your Sacred Space

After dedicating time and energy to creating, cleansing, decorating, and maintaining your sacred space, the most rewarding part is utilizing it in a way that enriches your spiritual practice.

This space is a sanctuary for growth, reflection, and connection with the divine, your higher self, and the universe. Here's how to make the most of your sacred space, integrating it into your daily life and spiritual routine.

Daily Meditation and Reflection

One of the simplest yet most profound ways to utilize your sacred space is for daily meditation and reflection. Set aside time each day to sit in your space, clear your mind, and meditate on your intentions, goals, or any spiritual queries you may have. This regular practice not only deepens your connection to your spiritual path but also strengthens the energies of your sacred space, making it even more potent over time.

Ritual Work

Your sacred space is the ideal setting for conducting rituals, spellwork, and other ceremonial practices. Whether marking the phases of the moon, celebrating Sabbats, or casting spells for specific intentions, doing so within the bounds of your sacred space adds depth and power to your work. The space's concentrated energy, aligned with your intentions and spiritual path, amplifies the efficacy of your rituals.

Journaling and Creative Expression

Consider using your sacred space as a haven for spiritual journaling or creative expression. Writing down your thoughts, experiences, and revelations can be a powerful practice, helping to manifest your intentions and clarify your spiritual journey. Similarly, engaging in creative activities like drawing, painting, or crafting within your sacred space can be a form of meditation and an expression of your innermost self.

Studying and Learning

For those dedicated to expanding their spiritual knowledge, your sacred space can serve as a peaceful study area. Reading sacred texts, exploring spiritual concepts, or learning about different practices in the tranquility of your sacred space can enhance your understanding and integration of these teachings into your practice.

Connecting with the Divine

Use your sacred space for prayer, divination, or communication with the divine, your ancestors, spirit guides, or deities. The focused energy of your space creates a conducive environment for receiving guidance, wisdom, and insights. Tools of divination such as tarot cards, runes, or pendulums can be particularly effective when used within the sacred space.

Rest and Rejuvenation

Sometimes, the best way to utilize your sacred space is simply to be in it, allowing yourself to rest, rejuvenate, and soak in its peaceful energy. Whether you're experiencing a period of turmoil, seeking solace, or needing to recharge your spiritual batteries, your sacred space offers a refuge.

Utilizing your sacred space is a dynamic process that evolves with your spiritual journey. Whether you engage in elaborate rituals, simple meditative practices or seek moments of quiet reflection, your sacred space is a versatile tool that supports and enhances your spiritual path. The key is to approach it with reverence, openness, and a willingness to explore the depths of your spirituality. Through regular use and engagement, your sacred space becomes more than just a physical location—it becomes a cornerstone of your spiritual life, a wellspring of energy, and a sacred portal to the divine.

3

TOOLS AND SYMBOLS OF THE CRAFT

In the rich tapestry of witchcraft, tools and symbols stand as a testament to the craft's deep roots in tradition, spirituality, and the natural world. These items, ranging from the simple to the ceremonial, are not merely accessories but vital components that bridge the mundane with the mystical, channeling energies and intentions in the practice of the craft. They serve as focal points for power, aids in ritual and spellwork, and as physical manifestations of the witch's connection to the divine, the elements, and the broader universe.

The significance of these tools and symbols extends beyond their practical applications, touching on the personal and collective unconscious. They carry the weight of centuries of lore, embodying the accumulated wisdom, beliefs, and experiences of countless practitioners who have come before. In this way, a wand, a chalice, or a pentagram is more than just an object; it is a link to the past, a symbol of continuity and community within the craft.

Moreover, these items are personal, with each witch selecting, creating, or adapting their tools to reflect their unique path and relationships with the forces they work with. This personalization transforms the tools from generic items into sacred objects, imbued with personal power and significance.

From the essential items found on altars around the world to the personal sigils crafted for specific intentions, we will uncover the layers of meaning and power these objects hold. Whether you are a seasoned practitioner or new to the craft, understanding the role and significance of these tools and symbols can deepen your practice, connect you to the broader currents of witchcraft, and enhance your spiritual journey.

Standard Tools of the Craft

Certain tools have become emblematic of the practice of witchcraft, each serving specific ritualistic or symbolic purposes. These tools not only aid in focusing and directing magical energy but also serve as physical representations of the witch's connection to the natural and spiritual worlds. Here's a closer look at some of the most common tools found within the craft and their significance.

The Altar

The altar is the heart of many witches' practice, a sacred space where magic is performed, and intentions are set. It acts as a physical representation of a witch's spiritual journey, often holding personal and symbolic items. The altar is typically dedicated to a deity, the elements, or the witch's higher self, serving as a focal point for ritual work. It can be as simple or elaborate as the practitioner desires, reflecting their personal aesthetics and spiritual path.

The Wand

A wand is a tool of invitation and invocations used to direct energy and summon entities during rituals. Traditionally made from wood, wands can also incorporate crystals, metal, or other materials that align with the witch's intentions. The choice of wood or other materials often corresponds to specific magical properties, such as oak for strength and endurance or willow for flexibility and intuition. The wand symbolizes the element of air, though in some traditions, it represents fire.

The Athame

The athame, a ceremonial knife, is a tool of protection and boundary setting. With its sharp blade, it's used to cast and cut the ritual circle, symbolically protecting the witch from negative energies and entities. Unlike mundane knives, the athame is not used for physical cutting but is a tool of energy direction. It typically represents the element of fire, symbolizing will and power, though in some paths it corresponds to air.

The Chalice

Representing the element of water, the chalice is a symbol of the divine feminine, the womb, and the ocean of the subconscious. It is used to hold water or wine during rituals, symbolizing the essence of life and the fluidity of magic. Drinking from the chalice can represent the internalization of divine energy or the act of sharing with the spirits or deities being honored.

The Pentacle

The pentacle, a disk or plate inscribed with a pentagram (five-pointed star), serves as a protective talisman and a tool for conjuration. It represents the element of earth, grounding magical work and symbolizing the material world. The pentacle is often used to consecrate other tools, objects, or ingredients by placing them upon it, imbuing them with the earth's stabilizing energies.

Candles

Candles are perhaps the most versatile tools in witchcraft. They are used for spellwork, meditation, and ambiance. Different colors are employed to align with specific intentions, such as green for prosperity, red for passion, or black for protection. The flame of a candle is symbolic of transformation, illumination, and the eternal dance between the spiritual and material realms.

Crystals and Stones

Crystals and stones are valued for their energetic properties, which are used in healing, protection, and enhancing other magical work. Each type of crystal or stone has its unique vibration and can be selected to support specific intentions. For example, amethyst is used for spiritual protection and insight, rose quartz is used for love and emotional healing, and clear quartz is used for the amplification of intent.

While common in the craft, these tools are personal to the practitioner's journey. The relationship with each tool grows over time, as does its effectiveness and significance within the witch's practice. Whether handmade, inherited, or acquired, these tools become imbued with personal energy and intent, serving as powerful aids in the transformative and revelatory processes of witchcraft.

Sacred Symbols in Witchcraft

Sacred symbols play a pivotal role in witchcraft, serving as focal points for magical intent, representations of divine energies, and keys to deeper mystical understanding. These symbols, rich in history and meaning, are woven into the fabric of many spells, rituals, and personal practices. They not only embody specific energies and concepts but also connect the practitioner to the broader currents of magical tradition and the collective unconscious. Here's an exploration of some of the most significant symbols within the craft and their layered meanings.

The Pentagram/Pentacle

The pentagram, a five-pointed star within a circle (when referred to as a pentacle), is one of the most recognizable symbols of witchcraft. Each point of the star represents an element—earth, air, fire, water—with the fifth point symbolizing spirit, thus illustrating the unity of all facets of existence. The pentacle is a potent symbol of protection, used to guard against negative energies and to invoke the elements during magical work. It stands as a testament to the balance and harmony of the universe and the witch's place within it.

The Triple Moon

Symbolizing the Goddess in her three aspects of maiden, mother, and crone, the Triple Moon emblem reflects the cycle of life, the phases of the moon, and the feminine divine. This symbol represents the full spectrum of female experience and wisdom, from youth and new beginnings through nurturing and stability to wisdom and the ending of cycles. It underscores the deep reverence for the feminine principle found in many witchcraft traditions and the connection to natural cycles and rhythms.

The Spiral

The spiral is a symbol of growth, evolution, and the cyclical nature of existence. Found in nature, from galaxies to the unfurling of ferns, the spiral speaks to the inherent order of the universe and the interconnectedness of all things. In witchcraft, it can represent the journey of life, the path of spiritual development, or the movement of energy in spells and rituals. The spiral invites contemplation of the mysteries of birth, growth, death, and rebirth.

The Eye of Horus

Borrowed from ancient Egyptian symbolism, the Eye of Horus is a powerful symbol of protection, health, and royal power. Within witchcraft, it is used to ward off evil, invoke divine watchfulness, and enhance psychic vision. This symbol embodies the idea of seeing beyond the visible world into the deeper truths and energies that animate existence.

The Ankh

The Ankh, another symbol adopted from ancient Egypt, represents life, eternal life, and the union of opposites. It is a key to mystical knowledge, symbolizing the balance between male and female, physical and spiritual, and the potential for eternal life. In witchcraft, the Ankh can be used to symbolize the life-giving power of water, the immortality of the soul, and the importance of balance in the universe.

Sigils

Sigils are magical symbols created for a specific intent, designed by the practitioner to manifest a particular goal or outcome. They are a form of magical shorthand, encoding the will of the witch into a visual form that can be charged with energy and released into the universe. Sigils embody the creative power of the witch to shape reality according to their will, using the language of symbols to communicate directly with the subconscious and the energies of the cosmos.

These sacred symbols, each with their rich histories and layers of meaning, offer powerful avenues for exploration, protection, and expression within the craft. Whether used in ritual, as part of a magical tool, or as a focus for meditation, they connect the practitioner to the deep currents of magical power and the ancient wisdom of the craft. Through these symbols, witches tap into the universal language of the mystical, weaving their intentions into the fabric of reality.

Creating and Consecrating Your Tools

The creation and consecration of tools are acts imbued with deep significance, transforming everyday objects into sacred vessels of magical intent. This process not only personalizes the tools, aligning them with the practitioner's energy and purpose but also dedicating them to the craft, ensuring they serve as effective conduits for magical work. Here's a guide on how to imbue your tools with personal power and purpose through creation and consecration.

Creating Your Tools

The creation of magical tools can be a personal and creative process, allowing for a deep connection to be forged between the tool and its wielder. Whether crafting a wand from a fallen branch, assembling a pentacle, or sewing a ritual robe, the act of creation is itself a ritual. Here are some considerations for creating your tools:

- **Material Selection:** Choose materials that resonate with the tool's intended use and your personal energies. Many practitioners prefer natural materials, such as wood, stone, or metal, for their inherent energies.
- **Timing:** Consider crafting your tools during specific lunar phases, days of the week, or even times of the day that align with the energy you wish to imbue in the

tool. For example, creating a protective amulet during the waning moon can enhance its power to banish negative energies.

- **Intention:** As you create, focus your intention on the purpose of the tool. Visualization, chants, or even playing music that aligns with your intention can infuse your creation with powerful energy.

Consecrating Your Tools

Consecration sets your tools apart for magical use, cleansing them of prior energies and dedicating them to your service in the craft. This sacred act not only purifies the tools but also aligns them with your personal energy and the divine, making them actual extensions of your will.

- **Cleansing:** Begin by cleansing your tools of any residual energy. This can be done through smoke cleansing with sage or incense, burying them in salt or earth, leaving them in moonlight, or using visualization techniques.
- **Ritual of Consecration:** Create a simple ritual that reflects your path and intentions. This might involve calling upon deities, elements, or spirits allied with your practice, anointing the tool with oils or water, and clearly stating the tool's purpose and dedication.
- **Charging:** After consecration, charge your tool with magical energy. This can be achieved through meditation, channeling energy from the earth or moon, or visualizing your energy flowing into the tool, activating its latent power.

DIY vs. Purchased Tools: Considerations

While there's a special connection to tools you've crafted with your own hands, not everyone has the means or ability to make all their tools. Purchased tools can be just as effective, provided they are chosen carefully and consecrated with personal intent. When selecting tools to buy:

- Choose items that speak to you energetically; you should feel a pull or connection to them.
- Cleanse and consecrate them as you would with any tool you've made yourself to align them with your energy and practice.
- If possible, personalize purchased tools by adding your own markings, decorations, or enhancements to strengthen the connection.

Creating and consecrating your tools are foundational practices in witchcraft. They imbue your instruments with the energies necessary for effective magical work. Whether handcrafted or carefully chosen, these tools become sacred extensions of your will and vital components of your practice, charged with your intentions and ready to aid you in manifesting your desires and aspirations.

Integrating Tools and Symbols into Practice

Incorporating tools and symbols into your witchcraft practice is a dynamic process that enhances the potency of your work, deepens your connection to the craft, and enriches your spiritual journey. These sacred objects and symbols, each imbued with specific energies and meanings, serve as conduits for your intent, grounding your magical practices in the physical world. Here's how to thoughtfully and effectively integrate these powerful elements into your daily and ritual practices.

Aligning Tools with Intentions

Begin by understanding the intrinsic energies and traditional uses of each tool and symbol. Align these with your intentions for your practice—whether for protection, healing, manifestation, or connection with the divine. For instance, use an oak wand for strength-related spells or a pentacle for grounding and protective rituals. By matching the tool to the intent, you amplify your magical work.

Daily Integration

Incorporate tools and symbols into your daily spiritual routine to strengthen your bond with them and enhance their efficacy in more formal rituals. This could involve:

- **Meditation with Crystals:** Hold a crystal with properties that align with your current focus or need, absorbing its energies as you meditate.
- **Candle Magic:** Light candles of specific colors to set intentions or create a focused ambiance for reflection.
- **Sigil Work:** Draw personal sigils on your skin, journals, or around your home as reminders of your goals and as active magical tools for manifestation.

Ritual Use

In ritual settings, each tool and symbol can be employed to perform specific functions, from casting circles with the athame to blessing offerings with the chalice. Use these items to draw down energy, mark sacred space, and direct your will. Incorporating symbols into your ritual space through altar cloths, decorations, or the arrangement of items can also enhance the ritual's thematic focus and energy.

Personalizing Symbols

While traditional symbols carry collective energies, personalizing these can tailor their power more closely to your path. This might involve creating your own sigils or adapting symbols to reflect your personal beliefs and experiences. Embed these personalized symbols in your tools, your sacred space, or even in wearable items to keep their energies and intentions close.

Balancing Tradition and Innovation

While the traditional meanings and uses of tools and symbols provide a valuable foundation, witchcraft is a living, evolving practice. Feel empowered to innovate and adapt the use of tools and symbols to suit your growing practice, intuition, and circumstances. This could mean reinterpreting a tool's use, combining symbols in new ways, or even discovering new tools and symbols through your work.

Integration through Creation and Care

Remember, creating or consecrating your tools and symbols is the first stepped in integrating them into your practice. Regularly cleansing and recharging these items not only maintains their efficacy but also reaffirms your connection to them, keeping the energies fresh and aligned with your intentions.

Integrating tools and symbols into your witchcraft practice is not just about the physical use of these items but about deepening your engagement with the craft itself. Through thoughtful selection, personalization, and daily ritual use, these sacred objects become extensions of your will, enriching your magical work with their power and presence. By honoring the traditional meanings while also listening to your intuition and adapting to your needs, you create a practice that is both rooted in tradition and vibrantly alive with personal significance.

4

UNDERSTANDING NATURAL ENERGIES

The practice of witchcraft is inherently intertwined with the rhythms and energies of the natural world. From the ebb and flow of the tides to the cycle of seasons and the celestial dance of the Moon and stars, each element of nature carries its unique energies and wisdom. For the witch, understanding and working with these natural energies is not just a practice but a profound way to connect with the essence of life itself. This introduction to working with natural energies explores the foundational concepts of moon phases, seasons, and elemental forces, providing a gateway to harmonizing your magical practice with the powerful currents of the Earth and the cosmos.

Historically, witches and practitioners of various spiritual paths have observed and revered the natural world, recognizing in it a mirror of the magical forces at work within and around us. Cultures across the globe have marked the passing of seasons with festivals and rituals, charted the stars for guidance, and looked to the Moon for signs of auspicious times. These practices underscore a universal understanding of the deep connection between the natural world and the spiritual realm.

In contemporary witchcraft, working with natural energies means attuning oneself to the subtle shifts in the environment, aligning rituals and spells with the phases of the Moon, the turning of the Wheel of the Year, and the elemental energies that permeate our world. Each aspect of nature offers unique opportunities for growth, reflection, and transformation, providing a rich tapestry of energies to draw upon in your practice.

Moon Phases

The Moon, with its enigmatic presence and luminous cycles, plays a pivotal role in witchcraft, serving as a celestial guide for timing spells, rituals, and personal reflection. Each lunar phase holds specific energies and symbolic meanings, influencing the ebb and flow of magical and natural currents. By aligning your practice with these lunar phases, you can harness their distinct powers to enhance your magical work and personal growth.

New Moon

The New Moon marks the beginning of the lunar cycle, a time of darkness that symbolizes new beginnings, fresh starts, and the planting of seeds—both literal and metaphorical. During this phase, witches focus on setting intentions, initiating new projects, and laying the groundwork for future endeavors. The New Moon is a blank slate, offering a potent opportunity for self-reflection and the setting of goals.

Rituals during this time might involve:

- Cleansing oneself of negative energies.
- Meditating on one's desires.
- Performing spells for new beginnings.

Waxing Moon

As the moon waxes, gradually increasing in light, it symbolizes growth, accumulation, and attraction. This is the ideal time to focus on spells and rituals that draw things toward you, such as love, prosperity, health, and success. The Waxing Moon's energy supports the building of momentum, making it a favorable time for efforts that require increase and expansion.

Practices during this phase might include:

- Crafting talismans to attract abundance.
- Performing affirmations for personal growth.
- Planting herbs and flowers that correspond with your intentions.

Full Moon

The Full Moon, with its radiant illumination, represents the culmination of energy, fulfillment, and realization. It is a time of heightened psychic awareness, emotional intensity, and powerful magical potential. Spells and rituals performed under the Full Moon benefit from its amplified energies, making it an ideal time for significant manifestations, healing, and divination. The Full Moon is also a moment of gratitude and celebration, acknowledging the fruition of intentions set during the New Moon. Celebratory rituals, charging crystals and tools in the moonlight, and performing spells for protection and purification are standard practices.

Waning Moon

Following the peak of the Full Moon, the Moon wanes, diminishing in light and symbolizing release, letting go, and the clearing of obstacles. This phase is conducive to banishing negative influences, ending unhealthy patterns, and detoxifying the physical and energetic bodies. The Waning Moon supports the process of decluttering one's life and making space for the new cycle ahead. Rituals include writing down burdens or obstacles and safely burning the paper, cleansing the home with smoke or saltwater, and performing spells for protection and release.

Aligning your witchcraft practice with the lunar phases allows you to work in harmony with the natural rhythms of the Universe, tapping into the specific energies and symbolic meanings of each phase. Whether setting intentions under the New Moon, attracting abundance with the Waxing Moon, manifesting desires at the Full Moon, or releasing negativity with the Waning Moon, the lunar cycle offers a robust framework for enhancing your magical work and personal development.

Seasons and the Wheel of the Year

The cycle of the seasons influences the energy of the Earth and all who live upon it, including the practices of those who follow the path of witchcraft. The Wheel of the Year, a representation of the annual cycle of seasonal festivals observed by many pagans, witches, and Wiccans, honors the changing face of nature and the deity aspects associated with each phase. This cyclical calendar not only marks agricultural and pastoral changes but also spiritual transitions, reflecting the eternal dance of life, death, and rebirth.

The Wheel of the Year

The Wheel of the Year consists of eight Sabbats: four solar festivals (the solstices and equinoxes) and four seasonal festivals (traditionally known as the "cross-quarter days") that fall approximately midway between the solstices and equinoxes.

Each Sabbat celebrates a specific aspect of the Earth's journey and offers unique energies for magical work and reflection.

- **Samhain** (October 31st- November 1st): Marking the end of the harvest and the beginning of winter, Samhain is a time to honor ancestors and those who have passed. It's believed the veil between worlds is thinnest during Samhain, making it an auspicious time for divination and communication with the spirit world.
- **Yule** (Winter Solstice, around December 21st): Celebrating the rebirth of the Sun, Yule is a festival of light amid the darkest time of the year. It symbolizes hope, renewal, and the promise of brighter days ahead.
- **Imbolc** (February 1st-2nd): Imbolc heralds the first signs of spring, focusing on purification and the lighting of fires to symbolize the returning warmth. It's a time for setting intentions for the coming year and initiating plans.
- **Ostara** (Spring Equinox, around March 21st): Marking the balance of day and night, Ostara celebrates new life, fertility, and the abundance of the burgeoning Earth. It's a time for sowing seeds both literally and metaphorically.
- **Beltane** (May 1st): Celebrating the peak of spring and the onset of summer, Beltane is a festival of fertility, fire, and abundance. It's a time for igniting desires and passions, marked by dancing around maypoles and jumping over fires.
- **Litha** (Summer Solstice, around June 21st): At the height of summer, Litha celebrates the Sun at its peak power, honoring the fullness of life and abundance of the Earth. It's a time for joy, celebration, and harnessing the Sun's potent energies.

- **Lammas or Lughnasadh** (August 1st): Marking the beginning of the harvest season, Lammas is a time of giving thanks for abundance and sharing with others. It's a period for reaping what has been sown, both in the fields and in personal endeavors.
- **Mabon** (Autumn Equinox, around September 21st): Celebrating the second harvest and the balance of light and dark, Mabon is a time for reflection, thanksgiving, and preparation for the dark half of the year. It's a period to enjoy the fruits of labor and to recognize the balance in all things.

Harnessing Seasonal Energies

Aligning your practice with the energies of the seasons means attuning to the natural rhythms of the Earth and incorporating the themes of each Sabbat into your rituals, spells, and personal reflection. This can involve:

- Creating altars adorned with symbols and items that reflect the current season's theme.
- Performing rituals that align with the Sabbat's energies, such as planting seeds at Ostara, lighting candles to welcome back the Sun at Yule, or offering gratitude for abundance at Lammas.
- Reflecting on personal growth, goals, and transformations, mirroring the cycle of death and rebirth seen in nature.

The Wheel of the Year offers a framework for understanding the natural energies at play throughout the seasons and integrating these into your magical practice. By celebrating the Sabbats, you honor the Earth's cycles and your connection to them, weaving the powerful energies of the seasons into the fabric of your spiritual journey.

Elements and Elemental Forces

The classical elements—Earth, Air, Fire, and Water—serve as the foundational pillars in many spiritual and magical practices, including witchcraft. Each element embodies unique characteristics, energies, and teachings, providing a framework through which practitioners can understand and interact with the natural world. By working with these elemental forces, witches can harness their energies to enhance spells, rituals, and personal growth.

Earth

Symbolism and Energy: Earth represents stability, fertility, and grounding. It is the element of solidity, endurance, and nourishment associated with the physical world, nature, and the body. Earth's energy is patient and reliable, embodying growth, prosperity, and abundance.

Working with Earth: Incorporate Earth into your practice by working with crystals, stones, herbs, and plants. Rituals focused on grounding, prosperity, and healing can draw on Earth's stable and nurturing energies. Creating a garden, even a small one, can be a powerful way to connect with Earth, as can spending time in nature, walking barefoot on the ground to feel its energy and support.

Air

Symbolism and Energy: Air represents intellect, communication, and knowledge. It is the element of movement, change, and inspiration associated with the mind, ideas, and dreams.

Air's energy is quick and dynamic, embodying clarity, perception, and the unseen forces that influence our world.

Working with Air: Engage with Air by practicing breathwork, using incense or smudging, and focusing on activities that stimulate the mind, such as writing, speaking, and divination. Spells for communication, travel, and knowledge can harness Air's swift and expansive qualities. Flying a kite or simply taking a moment to feel the wind on your skin can be simple yet profound ways to connect with Air.

Fire

Symbolism and Energy: Fire represents transformation, passion, and energy. It is the element of creation and destruction, associated with will, courage, and action. Fire's energy is intense and powerful, embodying change, motivation, and the drive to achieve one's desires.

Working with Fire: Incorporate Fire into your practice through candle magic, bonfires, and kitchen witchery. Focus on rituals that involve transformation, such as burning written intentions to release them to the Universe or cooking with the intention to infuse food with specific energies. Working with Fire requires respect and caution, acknowledging its potential for both creation and destruction.

Water

Symbolism and Energy: Water represents emotion, intuition, and healing. It is the element of fluidity, depth, and reflection associated with feelings, psychic abilities, and the subconscious mind. Water's energy is adaptable and flowing, embodying purification, love, and the mysteries of the inner self.

Working with Water: Engage with Water by incorporating baths, seashells, bowls of water, and aquatic plants into your rituals. Focus on spells and practices that involve healing, love, and psychic development. Spending time near bodies of water or simply taking a moment to drink water mindfully can help you connect with this element's soothing and cleansing energies.

Balancing the Elements

A balanced practice recognizes the importance of all four elements, understanding that each contributes essential energies to our lives and work. Many witches create altars featuring symbols of each element or cast circles calling upon their energies to create sacred, balanced space. Recognizing and honoring the elements within ourselves and in the world around us fosters harmony, deepens our connection to nature, and enhances our magical practice.

Working with the elements offers a way to tap into the primal forces that animate the Universe, providing a rich source of power, insight, and transformation. By understanding and integrating these elemental energies into your witchcraft, you align yourself with the rhythms of nature and the Universe, empowering your practice with the diverse and dynamic forces of Earth, Air, Fire, and Water.

Harnessing Natural Energies in Your Practice

Integrating natural energies into your witchcraft practice deepens your connection to the Earth. It enhances the potency of your magical work. The energies of the Moon, the shifting seasons, and the elemental forces provide a powerful foundation for spellcasting, rituals, and personal transformation. Here's how to harness these vibrant energies effectively in your practice.

Attuning to Lunar Energies

The Moon's cycle offers a rhythm for magical workings, providing different energies at each phase. Attuning your practice to these lunar energies involves:

- **Observation:** Begin by observing the Moon, noting how its phases impact your energy and emotions. Keeping a moon diary can help you track these influences over time.
- **Alignment:** Plan your spells and rituals in alignment with the lunar phases. Use the waxing Moon for attraction spells, the full Moon for manifestation and healing, and the waning Moon for banishing and release.
- **Rituals:** Create simple moon rituals to connect with lunar energy, such as moon bathing (sitting or meditating in the light of the full Moon) or charging water and crystals under the moonlight.

Embracing the Wheel of the Year

The cycle of the seasons reflects the cycle of life and offers unique energies for your magical work. To embrace these seasonal energies:

- **Celebrate Sabbats:** Mark the eight points of the Wheel of the Year with rituals or celebrations that honor the essence of each Sabbat, integrating seasonal symbols, foods, and activities.
- **Seasonal Altars:** Decorate your altar with items that reflect the current season, such as leaves in autumn for Mabon or flowers in spring for Ostara, to bring the energy of the changing seasons into your practice.
- **Nature Walks:** Regular walks in nature allow you to experience the shifting energies of the seasons

firsthand, deepening your connection to the Earth's cycles.

Working with Elemental Forces

The elements of Earth, Air, Fire, and Water offer diverse energies for magical work. Integrating these elemental forces can be achieved through:

- **Elemental Altars:** Create specific altars or spaces dedicated to each element, adorned with corresponding symbols and tools, such as a bowl of water for Water or a candle for Fire.
- **Elemental Spells:** Design spells and rituals that call upon the energies of specific elements, focusing on their unique attributes and powers. For example, use Water in spells for healing and emotional work or Fire for transformation and courage.
- **Daily Acknowledgment:** Incorporate a daily practice of acknowledging and thanking the elements, such as greeting the Sun (Fire) in the morning or feeling the ground beneath your feet (Earth) to cultivate a deeper relationship with these primal forces.

Creating Personal Rituals

Personal rituals that align with natural energies not only enhance your magical practice but also foster a profound connection to the natural world. Consider:

- **Customized Spells:** Develop spells that weave together lunar phases, seasonal energies, and elemental powers tailored to your specific intentions and needs.
- **Meditations:** Use guided or silent meditations to attune to the energy of the Moon, the current season,

or a chosen element, visualizing how these energies fill
and empower you.

- **Eco-Friendly Practices:** Incorporate eco-friendly
  practices into your rituals, such as using natural,
  biodegradable materials, to honor and protect the
  Earth as you draw upon its energies.

Harnessing natural energies requires mindfulness, respect, and
a willingness to listen to the subtle whispers of the Earth and
the cosmos. By attuning to these powerful currents and integrating them into your witchcraft practice, you align yourself
with the rhythms of nature, enhancing your spells, rituals, and
personal growth with the profound energies that flow through
all things.

Creating Rituals and Spells Aligned with Natural Forces

Designing rituals and spells that harness the profound energies
of natural forces—such as the Moon's phases, the cycle of
seasons, and elemental energies—enriches your magical practice with depth, resonance, and power. These natural forces
provide a vast palette from which to draw, enabling you to craft
work that is not only effective but also in harmony with the
rhythms of the Earth and the cosmos. Here's a guide to creating
rituals and spells that are aligned with these natural energies.

Aligning with the Moon

The lunar cycle offers a powerful template for spellcasting and
rituals, with each phase presenting unique opportunities:

- **New Moon Ritual for New Beginnings:** Use the
  energy of the new Moon to set intentions. Craft a ritual
  that involves writing down your goals on new pieces of
  paper, lighting a black or white candle to symbolize a

fresh start, and visualizing your intentions growing with the Moon's light. Bury the paper in a pot and plant a seed atop it, nurturing it as your intention grows.

- **Full Moon Spell for Manifestation:** The full Moon's radiant energy is perfect for manifestation. Gather symbols of what you wish to bring into your life and arrange them on a silver or white cloth under the full Moon. Use a moonstone crystal to amplify your intention, and chant or meditate on your desires, visualizing them coming to fruition. Close the spell by offering gratitude to the Moon.

Working with Seasonal Energies

Each season offers a unique backdrop for rituals and spells, reflecting the Earth's cycle of birth, life, death, and rebirth:

- **Samhain Ancestor Ritual:** At Samhain, when the veil between worlds is thinnest, create an altar honoring your ancestors with photographs, heirlooms, and offerings of food or drink they enjoyed. Light a black candle and invite their wisdom and guidance into your life through meditation or divination.
- **Ostara Ritual for Renewal and Growth:** Celebrate the spring equinox with a ritual that focuses on renewal and growth. Decorate your altar with spring flowers and light green and yellow candles to represent the burgeoning life, and write down aspects of your life you wish to grow or renew. Plant these wishes outside in your garden or in pots, symbolizing planting seeds for the future.

Harnessing Elemental Forces

Elemental energies provide a powerful means to ground your magical work in the physical world:

- **Fire Spell for Transformation:** Use fire's transformative power to catalyze change. Write down a habit or situation you wish to change on a piece of paper. Safely light a fire in a cauldron or fireplace, and as you burn the paper, visualize the unwanted energy being consumed and transformed into positive action. Use caution and respect whenever working with fire.
- **Water Ritual for Emotional Healing:** Water, with its healing and purifying qualities, is ideal for emotional healing. During the waxing Moon, gather water in a bowl and add sea salt, moonstone, and rose quartz. Holding your hands over the bowl, visualize your emotional wounds being cleansed and healed by the water. Pour the water over your hands or bathe in it, allowing the emotional pain to dissolve and flow away.

Integrating Natural Forces

When creating rituals and spells, consider the synergies between different natural forces. For example, a spell for personal growth might combine the waxing Moon's energy (for development), spring's vitality (for new beginnings), and the element of Earth (for grounding and stability). By thoughtfully combining these energies, your work gains layers of meaning and power.

Creating rituals and spells aligned with natural forces not only deepens your connection to the natural world but also enhances the effectiveness and resonance of your magical practice. By working in harmony with these powerful energies, you weave your intentions into the fabric of the Universe, supported by the elemental forces that animate life itself.

5

DEVELOPING YOUR INTUITION AND ABILITIES

Intuition and psychic abilities are intrinsic components of the human experience, offering a gateway to deeper understanding, guidance, and connection with the unseen world. Often regarded as the sixth sense, intuition is the subtle knowing without logical explanation, while psychic abilities extend this inner knowing to include phenomena such as clairvoyance, telepathy, and precognition. Far from being reserved for the few, these capabilities are dormant within all, awaiting awakening and cultivation.

This exploration into developing intuition and psychic abilities invites you on a journey of self-discovery, where the lines between the seen and unseen blur and the whispers of the Universe become discernible. It's a path that demands openness, patience, and a willingness to delve into the mysteries of your own consciousness. By honing these innate skills, you not only enhance your personal and spiritual growth but also tap into a wellspring of wisdom that can guide you through life's challenges and decisions.

Understanding and developing your intuition and psychic abilities involves recognizing the subtle energies and messages that constantly surround you. This chapter aims to provide practical exercises and insights to strengthen your intuitive and psychic senses, enabling you to navigate the world with an enhanced perception. Whether you're drawn to this path out of curiosity, a desire for personal growth, or the need for spiritual connection, the journey ahead offers profound opportunities for transformation and enlightenment.

In embracing these abilities, you'll learn to trust the guidance that flows from within, interpret the signs and omens presented by the Universe, and find a balance between the rational mind and the intuitive self. The goal is not to transcend the logical aspects of being but to harmonize logic and intuition, weaving them into a cohesive whole that resonates with truth and wisdom.

Exercises to Enhance Intuition and Psychic Abilities

Developing your intuition and psychic abilities is akin to strengthening a muscle—regular exercise and practice can significantly enhance these innate skills. Below are targeted exercises designed to awaken your intuitive senses and expand your psychic capabilities.

Meditative Practices

Mindful Breathing: To quiet the mind and center yourself, begin with essential mindful breathing. Sit comfortably, close your eyes, and focus on your breath. As you inhale and exhale, let go of distracting thoughts, allowing your mind to clear and become receptive to subtle intuitive impressions.

Visualization Meditation: Engage in visualization exercises to stimulate your third eye, the center of psychic vision. Visualize a radiant indigo light on your forehead, slowly expanding and brightening. Imagine this light enhancing your ability to see beyond the physical, opening your inner vision to intuitive insights and psychic phenomena.

Energy Sensing Exercises

Aura Reading: Practice sensing the aura, the energy field that surrounds all living beings. Start with plants or pets, focusing your attention on the space around them. Gradually, you may begin to sense colors, textures, or emotions emanating from their aura. With practice, extend this exercise to sensing human auras, noting any differences in energy or color you perceive.

Energy Shifting: Experiment with shifting energy within your own body to develop sensitivity to subtle energetic changes. Focus on directing energy to different parts of your body—your hands, your heart, your head—and notice the sensations that accompany these shifts, such as warmth, tingling, or lightness.

Divination Tools

Tarot or Oracle Cards: Begin a daily practice of drawing a card to enhance your intuitive interpretation skills. Don't rely solely on the guidebook; instead, pay attention to your immediate feelings, thoughts, or images that arise when you see the card. Over time, this practice can deepen your intuitive connection to the cards and the messages they hold.

Pendulum Work: Use a pendulum to practice receiving yes or no answers from your higher self or spirit guides. Ask questions to which you already know the answer to get a feel for how the pendulum responds. This exercise can help you trust your intuitive impulses and the subtle energies that influence the pendulum's movement.

Dream Work

Dream Journaling: Keep a dream journal by your bed to record any dreams or impressions as soon as you wake up. Dreams are a rich source of intuitive insight and psychic messages. Over time, review your journal for patterns, symbols, or messages that may be guidance from your subconscious or the spiritual realm.

Lucid Dreaming: As you become more attuned to your dreams, experiment with lucid dreaming—becoming conscious within your dream state and intentionally exploring the dream world. Before going to sleep, set an intention to become aware you're dreaming and use this state as a play-ground for psychic exploration.

Psychic Reading Practice

Blind Reading: Exchange objects with a friend (such as a piece of jewelry) and practice reading the energy or history of the object without prior knowledge. Share your impressions, however vague, and validate with each other to build confidence in your psychic insights.

Intuitive Development Group

Join or create an intuitive development group where you can practice psychic exercises, share experiences, and validate each other's insights in a supportive environment. Group energy can significantly amplify psychic experiences and provide diverse perspectives on interpreting intuitive information.

Incorporating these exercises into your routine can gradually awaken and enhance your intuition and psychic abilities. Remember, patience and consistent practice are vital to developing these skills. Trust in your natural abilities and be open to the journey of discovery that unfolds.

Understanding and Interpreting Signs and Omens

The Universe communicates with us in myriad ways, often sending signs and omens that guide, warn, or affirm. These messages can manifest in the natural world, in synchronicities, or through intuitive insights, requiring a keen sense of awareness and openness to interpret. Understanding and analyzing these signs involves recognizing their occurrence, deciphering their symbolism, and applying their guidance to our lives.

Recognizing Signs

Signs and omens are all around us, but not every coincidence or unusual event carries a message. The key to recognizing meaningful signs involves several factors:

- **Frequency:** A sign often repeats in various forms. If a particular animal, number, or symbol keeps appearing in your life, it might be carrying a message.
- **Timing:** A sign's relevance is often linked to its timing, appearing when you're facing a decision, challenge, or transition.
- **Emotional Resonance:** Signs often evoke a noticeable emotional or physical response, such as a feeling of peace, excitement, or a sense of knowing.

Symbolism and Personal Meaning

Symbols can carry universal meanings but often hold personal significance shaped by our experiences, beliefs, and cultural background. Developing a personal lexicon of symbols involves:

- **Research:** Learn about the traditional meanings of symbols, animals, numbers, and other omens in various spiritual and cultural contexts.
- **Intuition:** When you encounter potential signs, pay attention to your feelings and thoughts. Your intuition can provide clues about their personal relevance and meaning.
- **Journaling:** Keep a journal of signs and your interpretations, noting any patterns or themes that emerge over time. This record can become a valuable tool for understanding your unique symbolic language.

Context and Intuition

The context in which a sign appears is crucial to its interpretation. A black cat crossing your path might have one meaning on a day when you're pondering a risky decision and another when you're exploring your shadow self. Consider the following when interpreting signs:

- **Current Life Situations:** Reflect on your current challenges, questions, or themes in your life. How might the sign relate to these?
- **Cultural and Personal Associations:** Consider both the broader cultural symbolism and your personal associations with the sign.
- **Gut Feeling:** Trust your initial gut reaction to the sign. Often, our first intuitive understanding is the most accurate.

Balancing Skepticism and Belief

Interpreting signs and omens requires a balance between skepticism and belief. While remaining open to messages from the

Universe, it's essential to maintain discernment, avoiding the tendency to see signs in everything or to interpret them in ways that align only with our desires. Ask for clarification if a sign's message is unclear, and be prepared to wait for further guidance.

Integrating Signs into Your Practice

Once you've interpreted a sign or omen, integrating its message into your life or practice can involve:

- **Reflection:** Spend time in meditation or contemplation, considering the sign's implications and how it might guide your actions or decisions.
- **Ritual:** Create a small ritual to acknowledge the sign and express gratitude for the guidance received, committing to any action or change it suggests.
- **Continued Observation:** Remain attentive to further signs or confirmations, primarily after you've acted on the message received.

Understanding and interpreting signs and omens is a personal process, enriched by patience, attentiveness, and a willingness to engage with the mysteries of the Universe. By cultivating these skills, you open yourself to profound guidance and insights, deepening your connection to the natural world and the spiritual path.

Balancing the Logical Mind with Intuitive Wisdom

The journey of spiritual and personal growth often navigates the delicate balance between the logical mind and intuitive wisdom. Our rational mind allows us to analyze, reason, and make decisions based on concrete information. At the same time, our intuition offers a more subtle, often instantaneous understanding that bypasses analytical reasoning. Both are invaluable assets, and learning to balance these aspects can significantly enhance decision-making processes, creative endeavors, and spiritual practices. Here's how to cultivate harmony between the rational and the intuitive.

The Role of the Logical Mind

The logical mind is our analytical powerhouse, processing information, solving problems, and planning based on past experiences and learned knowledge. It's crucial for everyday functioning and critical thinking, enabling us to navigate the world with discernment and make informed decisions. However, when overemphasized, it can lead to doubt, over-thinking, and disconnect from the intuitive self.

- **Awareness:** Recognize when the logical mind is dominating, excluding intuition. Awareness is the first step in creating balance.
- **Appreciation:** Value the logical mind for the structure and stability it brings to your life, understanding that it is part of the balance rather than an adversary to intuition.

Cultivating Intuition

Intuition is often described as a gut feeling or a knowing without knowing why. It can guide us toward our true path, resonate with truth, and connect us more with others and the Universe.

- **Meditation and Mindfulness:** Regular meditation and mindfulness practices can quiet the chatter of the logical mind, creating space for intuition to emerge.

- **Intuitive Practices:** To strengthen this natural ability, regularly engage in practices that stimulate intuition, such as tarot reading, journaling, or working with dreams.
- **Trust and Act:** Trusting your intuition and acting on its guidance, even in small ways, reinforces its validity and strengthens your confidence in using it.

Harmony Between Mind and Intuition

Achieving harmony between the logical mind and intuitive wisdom involves recognizing the value of both and creating a practice that honors each aspect.

- **Integration:** In decision-making, consider both the logical analysis and the intuitive sense of the situation. Ask yourself, "What do I think?" and "What do I feel?" about the decision at hand.
- **Mindfulness Practices:** Techniques such as mindfulness can help you become more aware of the moment when intuition speaks, allowing you to acknowledge and integrate this insight with logical reasoning.
- **Journaling:** Keep a journal documenting instances where you followed your intuition, noting the outcomes. This can validate the power of your intuitive wisdom and encourage a more balanced approach in the future.

Case Studies: Integration in Action

Reflecting on stories or case studies where individuals successfully combined logical reasoning with intuitive insight can offer practical examples of this balance in action. Whether in solving complex problems, navigating career decisions, or creating art, these stories highlight the dynamic interplay between analysis and intuition, offering inspiration for cultivating balance in your own life.

Balancing the logical mind with intuitive wisdom is not about diminishing one in favor of the other but about recognizing and valuing both as essential components of a holistic approach to life. This balance allows for more nuanced understanding and decision-making, enriching both your spiritual journey and everyday experiences. By honoring and integrating these complementary aspects of your being, you open yourself to a more rounded and profound engagement with the world.

6

SPELLCRAFT AND RITUALS

Spellcraft and rituals form the essence of the witch's practice, a profound dialogue between the practitioner and the unseen forces that shape our reality. This ancient art blends intention, natural energies, and symbolic actions to manifest change, both within the outer world and the inner landscapes of our being. It's a practice as varied as the practitioners themselves, each spell and ritual a unique expression of desire, belief, and personal power. At the heart of spellcraft lies the understanding that we are connected to the cosmos and capable of influencing the web of existence through our will and intention.

This chapter introduces the fundamental concepts of creating and casting spells, guiding you through the process of designing rituals that resonate with your individual path, whether for self-growth, protection, or manifesting your deepest desires. It also delves into the ethics and responsibilities inherent in wielding such power, underscoring the importance of intentionality, respect, and the awareness of the broader consequences of our magical actions.

Spellcraft and rituals are not just mechanisms for enacting change; they are sacred acts of co-creation with the Universe, requiring clarity, focus, and a harmonious alignment with natural forces. By engaging in these practices, we step into a realm where the seen and unseen meet, where the boundaries between worlds blur, and where our true potential as creators and healers is revealed.

As we embark on this exploration, remember that the power of spellcraft and rituals lies not in the complexity of the actions or the rarity of the materials used but in the depth of the connection forged between the practitioner, the divine, and the natural world. Through this practice, we learn not just to speak the language of magic but to listen to the responses it elicits, navigating the intricate dance of cause and effect, give and take that defines the Universe. Welcome to the journey of spellcraft and rituals, where every word, every gesture, and every intention can open doors to new possibilities and transformations.

Fundamentals of Creating and Casting Spells

Creating and casting spells is an art that weaves together intention, natural energies, and symbolic actions to manifest desired outcomes. At its core, spellcraft is about aligning your will with the Universe to bring about change. Here's a foundational guide to understanding the components and processes involved in effective spellcasting.

Components of a Spell

I. **Intention:** The heart of every spell is the intention— the clear, focused desire you wish to manifest. It should be specific, positive, and stated in the present tense as though it's already happening.

2. **Timing:** The timing of a spell can significantly enhance its effectiveness. This includes considering lunar phases (e.g., new Moon for beginnings, full Moon for fruition), days of the week, and astrological considerations to align with the energies that best support your intention.

3. **Symbols and Correspondences:** Symbols, colors, herbs, stones, and other items carry specific energies and meanings. Selecting materials that correspond with your intention can amplify the spell's power.

4. **Words:** Words, whether spoken aloud, whispered, or written, act as a vehicle for your intention. Crafting a chant, rhyme, or affirmation can help focus your will and direct energy.

5. **Actions:** Physical actions, such as lighting a candle, assembling a charm, or anointing with oils, ground the spell in the material world, bridging the gap between thought and reality.

Steps for Casting a Spell

1. **Preparation:** Begin by grounding and centering yourself. Create a sacred space where you feel protected and focused, and gather all the materials you'll need for the spell.

2. **Setting Intention:** Clearly define your intention. Please write it down or spend a few moments visualizing it in vivid detail, feeling the emotions associated with its fulfillment.

3. **Calling Upon Energies:** Depending on your practice, you may call upon deities, spirits, elements, or simply the Universe to aid in your spellcasting. This step is about connecting with powers more significant than yourself to support your intention.

4. **Raising Energy:** Energy can be raised through visualization, dance, chanting, drumming, or other methods. Picture your energy intertwining with the energies you've called upon, building in intensity and focus.

5. **Directing Energy:** Direct the raised energy towards your intention. Use your words, actions, and visualization to focus the energy on the symbols and items representing your desire.

6. **Release and Closure:** Release the energy to do its work in the world. Visualize sending it out into the Universe or into the item you're enchanting. Close the spell by thanking any energies or entities you called upon, grounding any excess energy, and affirming that your intention will manifest.

7. **Follow-up Actions:** Align your mundane actions with your magical intention. For example, if you cast a spell for a new job, continue to apply for jobs and attend interviews.

Tips for Successful Spellcasting

- **Clarity and Focus:** Be clear about what you want to achieve and stay focused during the spell. Distractions can dilute the energy directed toward your intention.
- **Belief and Openness:** Belief in your power and the effectiveness of your spell. Be open to outcomes, recognizing that the Universe might fulfill your intention in unexpected ways.
- **Ethical Considerations:** Consider the moral implications of your spell. Avoid spells that manipulate others' free will or cause harm.

Crafting and casting spells is a personal and transformative process. By understanding the fundamentals and approaching spellcraft with respect, intention, and an open heart, you tap into the ancient art of manifesting change—both within yourself and in the world around you.

Designing Rituals for Self-Growth, Protection, and Manifesting Desires

Rituals are structured, intentional actions imbued with symbolic meaning, designed to facilitate change, growth, and protection. They are the sacred practices through which we connect more with the energies of the Universe to manifest our desires, protect our space, and foster personal development. Below are guidelines for designing rituals tailored to these specific aims.

Rituals for Self-Growth

Self-growth rituals focus on inner development, healing, and transformation. They are compelling during times of transition or when seeking to overcome personal challenges.

- **Creating a Self-Growth Ritual:** Begin by defining the area of growth or healing you wish to focus on. It could be confidence, emotional healing, or spiritual awakening. Select symbols, elements, and actions that resonate with this intention. For example, a butterfly for transformation, water for emotional healing, or a mirror for self-reflection.
- **Sample Ritual:** On the night of a waxing moon, symbolizing growth, create a sacred space adorned with blue candles for healing and a small bowl of water. Write down aspects of yourself you wish to heal or develop on pieces of paper. One by one, read these

aloud, and then dissolve them in the water, visualizing your obstacles dissolving and your true self emerging. Close the ritual by meditating on your innate potential for growth.

Rituals for Protection

Protection rituals aim to safeguard an individual, space, or object from negative influences or energies. These rituals create energetic boundaries, invoking peace and safety.

- **Creating a Protection Ritual:** Identify what you wish to protect and the nature of the protection needed. Gather symbols of strength and safety, such as black tourmaline for warding off negativity, salt for purification, or an image of a guardian or deity that represents protection to you.
- **Sample Ritual:** To protect your home, mix sea salt and water, charging it with your intention for protection. Sprinkle this solution around your home's perimeter, doorways, and windows while visualizing an impenetrable barrier of light surrounding your space. Light a black candle to absorb negativity and recite a mantra of protection. Finish by placing protective amulets or symbols near entry points.

Rituals for Manifesting Desires

These rituals are focused on bringing specific desires or goals into reality. They harness the power of intention, visualization, and the appropriate correspondences to attract what you seek.

- **Creating a Manifestation Ritual:** Clearly define your desire. Choose correspondences that align with your goal, such as green candles for prosperity, rose quartz for love, or images that represent your desire. Timing can also enhance your ritual; for example, a waxing moon phase for growth or abundance.

- **Sample Ritual:** To manifest a new job, gather symbols of the career you desire and a green candle for prosperity. Write a detailed letter to the Universe, outlining your ideal job and why you're a perfect fit. Light the candle, read your letter aloud, and then burn it, allowing the smoke to carry your intentions to the Universe. Carry a piece of citrine with you as a talisman until your job manifests.

Balancing the Logical Mind with Intuitive Wisdom in Ritual Design

When designing your rituals, balance the logical mind's planning and structure with the intuitive wisdom that speaks to the soul's needs. Trust your instincts about what symbols, elements, and actions feel right, allowing your intuition to guide the creative process. This balance ensures that your rituals are not only practical but meaningful and personal.

Rituals are a powerful way to actively engage with the energies of the Universe to facilitate self-growth, protection, and the manifestation of desires. By thoughtfully combining intention, symbolism, and action, you create a focused energy that propels you toward your goals, grounded in the knowledge that you are the architect of your reality.

Ethics and Responsibilities of Spellcasting

The practice of spellcasting carries with it a significant ethical responsibility. As spellcasters wield energies to manifest changes in the physical and spiritual realms, they must consider the broader implications of their work. Ethical spellcasting is rooted in mindfulness, respect, and a deep under-standing of the interconnectedness of all beings. This section explores the foundational ethical considerations and responsi-bilities inherent in spellcasting.

The Wiccan Rede and the Rule of Three

Many practitioners adhere to the Wiccan Rede, "An it harm none, do what ye will," as a guiding principle for ethical conduct. This statement emphasizes the importance of causing no harm through one's magical actions. Closely related is the Rule of Three, or the Threefold Law, which suggests that what-ever energy a person puts out into the world, whether positive or negative, will return to them threefold. Together, these prin-ciples encourage practitioners to consider the consequences of their spells and to strive for actions that promote positivity and harmony.

Consent and Respect

One of the most critical ethical considerations in spellcasting is the matter of consent. Casting spells on or for others without their explicit permission can infringe upon their free will and autonomy. It is crucial to respect each individual's sovereignty and to obtain their consent before performing any magic that directly affects them. This respect extends to working with spir-itual entities or deities, where offering respect and seeking permission or guidance is equally important.

Responsibility for Outcomes

Spellcasters must acknowledge their responsibility for the outcomes of their spells, both intended and unintended. While the Universe might interpret and fulfill intentions in unex-pected ways, practitioners should approach spellcasting with clarity, focus, and an understanding of the potential ripple effects of their work. This responsibility also involves being prepared to accept and address any harmful consequences that may arise, seeking to rectify the harm, and learning from the experience.

Ethical Considerations in Spell Design

Designing spells with ethical considerations in mind involves:

- **Avoiding Manipulative Intentions:** Spells should not seek to control or manipulate others but instead focus on personal growth, protection, and positive manifestations that do not infringe on others' will.
- **Positive Framing:** Frame spells in positive terms, focusing on attracting what you desire rather than banishing or negating what you don't. This positive approach aligns better with ethical practices and the principle of causing no harm.
- **Environmental Impact:** Consider the environmental impact of your spellcasting materials and practices. Use ethically sourced, sustainable materials whenever possible, and perform rituals in ways that do not harm the Earth.

Continuous Learning and Reflection

Ethical spellcasting is a journey of continuous learning and reflection. Engage in ongoing education about different magical traditions and moral perspectives. Reflect on your practices and their outcomes, being open to evolving your understanding of what it means to cast spells ethically. This reflective practice ensures that your spellcasting remains aligned with a commitment to do good and to contribute positively to the world.

Spellcasting is a powerful tool for change, growth, and connection. By embracing the ethical responsibilities that accompany this practice, practitioners can ensure that their work promotes well-being, respects autonomy, and contributes to the balance and harmony of the Universe. Ethical spellcasting is not only about adhering to external principles but also about cultivating an inner compass that guides you toward actions that uplift and heal, reflecting the highest ideals of witchcraft and spirituality.

7

THE WITCH'S SABBATS AND ESBATS

The Wheel of the Year, a cycle ingrained in the tapestry of witchcraft and various pagan traditions, serves as a symbolic representation of the changing seasons and the natural rhythm of the Earth's journey around the Sun. It marks the passage of time, not through the pages of a calendar, but through the ebb and flow of natural energies, agricultural cycles, and the celestial dance that influences both the Earth and its inhabitants. This cyclical wheel is punctuated by eight Sabbats, each celebrating significant transitions in the seasonal year, from the deep slumber of winter to the abundant life of summer and back again.

The Sabbats include four solar festivals — the solstices and equinoxes — marking the Sun's highest and lowest points on the horizon and the balance of day and night. These are Yule (Winter Solstice), Ostara (Spring Equinox), Litha (Summer Solstice), and Mabon (Autumn Equinox). Interspersed are four agricultural and pastoral festivals — Imbolc, Beltane, Lammas, and Samhain — that celebrate milestones of the farming year, such as planting, growth, harvest, and the end of the growing season.

Each Sabbat carries its own unique energy and significance, rooted in ancient traditions and lore. These festivals offer a moment to pause and reflect on the impermanence of life, the beauty of nature, and the continuous cycle of death and rebirth. They are times of celebration, reflection, and renewal, where witches and pagans alike honor the Earth, the Sun, and the natural forces that sustain life.

Celebrating the Sabbats in the modern era connects practitioners to the rhythms of nature and our ancestors who once lived by these cycles, relying on them for survival. It's a practice that transcends mere tradition, becoming a profound way to live in harmony with the Earth and its cycles. As we turn the Wheel of the Year, we are reminded of the interconnectedness of all things, the ever-present cycle of change, and the enduring cycle of life, death, and rebirth.

Whether celebrated in grand gatherings or quiet, solitary rituals, the Sabbats offer a pathway to deepen our connection with the natural world, the divine, and ourselves, marking our place in the endless cycle of the year.

Celebrating the Lunar Cycles with Esbats

Esbats are the celebrations and rituals that honor the Moon's phases, providing a rhythmic counterpart to the solar-focused Sabbats of the Wheel of the Year. While Sabbats celebrate the Earth's relationship with the Sun, Esbats are dedicated to the Moon and its cycle, embodying the feminine aspect of the divine, the subconscious, and the ebb and flow of energy and emotions. These lunar celebrations offer witches and pagans a more frequent cadence of observance, typically focusing on the full Moon but also including the new Moon and other phases, each holding its unique energy and significance.

The Significance of Lunar Energy

The Moon, with its monthly cycle of waxing and waning, mirrors the cycle of life, growth, decline, and rebirth. Its phases influence the natural world, from the tides of the ocean to the growth of plants, and symbolize the cycle of our own endeavors and spiritual journey. By aligning with lunar energy through Esbats, practitioners can harness these natural rhythms for introspection, manifestation, release, and renewal.

Celebrating Full Moon Esbats

The full Moon, with its bright illumination, represents the culmination of energy, fruition, and completion. It's a potent time for spellcasting, divination, and charging magical tools, as well as for releasing what no longer serves you.

- **Rituals and Activities:** Full moon rituals often involve gathering in circles to raise energy, performing spells for manifestation, and engaging in divination practices. Solitary witches might charge their crystals and tools under the moonlight, take a cleansing moonlit bath, or meditate to connect with their intuition and the divine.
- **Creating Moon Water:** A simple but powerful Esbat practice involves leaving water out under the full Moon to charge it with lunar energy. This moon water can then be used for cleansing, as an offering, or in spellwork.

Honoring the New Moon

The new Moon, representing new beginnings, is a time for setting intentions for the lunar cycle ahead. It's a period of darkness, symbolizing potential and the planting of seeds (both literal and metaphorical).

- **Rituals and Activities:** New moon rituals might include writing down intentions, planting seeds as a symbolic act of manifestation, or quiet reflection on desires and goals. Some practitioners also use this time for shadow work, exploring the subconscious and aspects of the self that are usually hidden.

Working with Waxing and Waning Phases

The waxing Moon, growing fuller, symbolizes attraction and building energy. It is ideal for spells and rituals focused on bringing things into your life, such as love, prosperity, and growth. The waning Moon, as it diminishes, supports banishment, release, and letting go, helping to clear obstacles and negative energies.

- **Rituals and Activities:** Use the waxing Moon for attraction spells or to start new projects with the intention of growth. During the waning Moon, focus on cleansing your space, purifying your aura, and releasing habits, relationships, or situations that no longer serve your highest good.

Integrating Esbats into Solo Practice

Celebrating Esbats in solitary practice allows for deep personal reflection and a direct connection with lunar energies. Customize your rituals to reflect your individual path, using symbols, deities, and elements that resonate with you. Keeping a lunar journal can help track your experiences, insights, and the progression of your intentions throughout the lunar cycle.

Esbats offer a beautiful opportunity to align with the natural world, honoring the divine feminine and the rhythms of the Moon. Whether through grand rituals or simple acts of reflection, celebrating the lunar cycles enriches the spiritual practice, connecting us more with the cycles of nature and our own inner cycles of growth and renewal.

Solo Rituals and Celebrations for the Sabbats

The Wheel of the Year turns, bringing with it the changing energies of the seasons, each marked by its own Sabbat. For the solitary witch, these times offer opportunities for personal reflection, renewal, and celebration. Crafting solo rituals that resonate with the essence of each Sabbat not only honors these seasonal shifts but also deepens one's connection to the natural world and the self.

Samhain (October 31st)

Ritual Focus: Honoring ancestors and reflecting on cycles of death and rebirth.

- **Ancestor Altar:** Create a small altar dedicated to your ancestors. Decorate it with photographs, mementos, and offerings like bread, apples, or wine. Light a black or white candle and spend some time remembering your loved ones, perhaps sharing stories or messages aloud.
- **Divination:** Samhain is a potent time for divination. Use tarot cards, runes, or a pendulum to seek guidance for the year ahead. Focus on personal transformation and paths to growth.

Yule (Winter Solstice, around December 21st)

Ritual Focus: Celebrating the return of light and setting intentions for the coming year.

- **Sunrise Vigil:** Rise early to greet the dawn on Yule, lighting candles or a fire to welcome back the Sun. Reflect on the Sun's journey and your own parallel path of growth and renewal.
- **Intention Setting:** Write down your hopes and intentions for the New Year. Burn the paper in your Yule fire or candle flame, releasing your wishes to the Universe.

Imbolc (February 1st)

Ritual Focus: Welcoming the first signs of spring and purifying for the new cycle.

- **Candle Magic:** Light multiple candles to symbolize the returning light. Meditate on purification and renewal, visualizing the light dispelling the shadows within.
- **Brigid's Cross:** Craft Brigid's cross from reeds or grass as a protective amulet for the coming year, inviting Brigid's blessings of vitality and healing.

Ostara (Spring Equinox, around March 21st)

Ritual Focus: Celebrating new growth and balance.

- **Planting Seeds:** Physically plant seeds as a symbolic act of manifestation for your goals. As you plant, visualize your intentions growing with the plants.
- **Equilibrium Meditation:** Reflect on balance, meditating on areas of your life that require harmony.

Use this time to align your inner self with the equilibrium of day and night.

Beltane (May 1st)

Ritual Focus: Igniting passion and celebrating fertility.

- **Fire Ritual:** Safely light a small fire or candle to symbolize the Beltane fire. Write down what you wish to manifest, focusing on passion and vitality, and pass the paper through the flame, visualizing your desires coming to life.
- **Nature Walk:** Take a walk in nature, observing the burgeoning life around you. Collect flowers or greenery to decorate your altar or living space, embracing the fertility and abundance of the season.

Litha (Summer Solstice, around June 21st)

Ritual Focus: Honoring the Sun at its peak and the abundance of summer.

- **Sun Water:** Place a bowl of water in direct sunlight to create sun water. Use this charged water for blessings, purification, or as an offering. Reflect on the abundance and strength in your life, giving thanks for the light.
- **Solar Meditation:** Meditate under the Sun, absorbing its warmth and vitality. Contemplate your personal power and how you can shine your light in the coming months.

Lammas (August 1st)

Ritual Focus: Giving thanks for the first harvest and acknowledging achievements.

- **Bread Baking:** Bake bread from scratch, infusing it with gratitude for the abundance in your life. Break bread in a ritual act, offering a portion to the Earth as thanks.
- **Harvest List:** Write a list of your achievements and things you are grateful for from the past year. Reflect on these blessings, acknowledging your hard work and growth.

Mabon (Autumn Equinox, around September 21st)

Ritual Focus: Celebrating the second harvest and the balance of light and dark.

- **Gratitude Ritual:** Create an altar with symbols of the harvest (fruits, grains, autumn leaves). Light a candle and meditate on the things you're grateful for, offering thanks for the bounty in your life.
- **Balancing Stones:** Stack stones or balance them in a meaningful formation as a meditation on balance and stability. Reflect on areas of your life that are in harmony and those that may need attention.

Each Sabbat offers a unique opportunity for the solitary practitioner to connect with the cyclical energies of nature. These solo rituals and celebrations allow for personal reflection, growth, and gratitude, deepening your practice and your connection to the Wheel of the Year.

Celebrating Esbats: Solo Full Moon Rituals

Esbats, particularly those that celebrate the full Moon, are special moments in the witch's calendar, providing opportunities for reflection, manifestation, and connection with lunar energies. The full Moon, with its powerful influence over the Earth and its inhabitants, is a time of heightened intuition, emotional clarity, and magical potency. Here are rituals and practices designed for solitary witches to celebrate Esbats and harness the energies of the full Moon.

Creating Sacred Space

Begin by cleansing your space with sage, Palo Santo, or sound vibrations to purify the area and create a sacred environment. You may choose to cast a circle, calling upon the elements and any deities or spirits you work with to protect and sanctify your space.

Moon Water Ritual

- **Materials Needed:** A clear glass jar or bowl, spring water, and optional crystals like moonstone or clear quartz.
- **Ritual:** Fill your vessel with spring water, and if you are using it, place your cleansed crystals inside. Set the water in a spot where it can bask in the moonlight overnight. As you do this, speak your intentions into the water, asking the Moon to bless it with its qualities (such as clarity, intuition, or emotional healing). The following day, retrieve your moon water. Use it to anoint yourself for clarity and blessing, in spellwork, or as an offering.

Full Moon Meditation for Release and Manifestation

- **Preparation:** Find a comfortable, quiet space where you can see the Moon or feel its presence. Have a list of things you wish to release and another list of what you want to attract.
- **Ritual:** Begin by focusing on your breath, allowing your body to relax and your mind to clear. Visualize the Moon's rays enveloping you, charging you with light and energy.
- First, focus on the things you wish to release. One by one, imagine handing each item on your list to the Moon, asking it to take these burdens from you. Visualize them dissolving in the Moon's light.
- Next, turn your focus to your manifestations. Visualize each desire in turn, seeing it as vividly as possible and feeling the emotions of its fulfillment. Imagine planting these desires in the moonlit soil, knowing they are nurtured by the Moon's energy.
- Conclude by expressing gratitude to the Moon and slowly returning to your physical surroundings, carrying the Moon's blessings with you.

Candle Spell for Intuition

- **Materials Needed:** A silver or blue candle (for intuition), a carving tool, and oil for dressing the candle (lavender or jasmine work well).
- **Ritual:** Carve symbols or words related to your intention for enhanced intuition into your candle. Dress the candle with your chosen oil, focusing on your desire for clarity and insight. Light the candle, gazing into the flame and visualizing your intuitive abilities expanding. Meditate on this vision until the

candle burns down or for as long as you feel comfortable. Snuff out the candle to conclude, or let it burn entirely if it is safe to do so.

Charging Magical Tools

The full Moon is an optimal time to charge your magical tools, crystals, and amulets with lunar energy. Lay your items out where they can absorb the moonlight, either outdoors or on a windowsill. As you place each item, speak your intention for it, asking the Moon to bless and empower it. Leave them overnight to bask in the Moon's glow, and then collect them in the morning, giving thanks for the Moon's blessing.

These solo full moon rituals offer a way to connect with the lunar energies, providing a framework for release, manifestation, and empowerment. As with all rituals, feel free to adapt these practices to suit your personal path, intuition, and the specific energies of each full Moon. Celebrating Esbats alone allows for an individual experience, fostering growth and understanding as you walk your solitary witch's path under the Moon's watchful gaze.

Integrating Sabbats and Esbats into Solo Practice

Integrating the celebration of Sabbats and Esbats into your solo practice enriches your spiritual journey, aligning you with the natural rhythms of the Earth and the Moon. These observances offer structured moments of reflection, connection, and intention-setting throughout the year. For the solitary witch, these times can become personal milestones of growth, transformation, and empowerment. Here's how to weave the magic of Sabbats and Esbats into your solo practice in meaningful and fulfilling ways.

Creating Personal Traditions

One of the joys of solitary practice is the freedom to create personal traditions that resonate with your unique spiritual path. Start by exploring the historical and symbolic meanings of each Sabbat and Esbat, and then consider how these themes relate to your life and aspirations. Craft rituals, ceremonies, and celebrations that reflect your personal connection to these energies. Over time, these practices will evolve into rich traditions that hold profound personal significance.

- **Sabbat Example:** For Samhain, you might create a yearly tradition of a silent supper to honor the ancestors, followed by a personal divination session to gain insight into the year ahead.
- **Esbat Example:** For full moon Esbats, establish a ritual of Moon gazing or walking, using this time to meditate on your desires and the manifestations you wish to see in your life.

Honoring the Lunar Cycle

Esbats provide a monthly opportunity for reflection and intention-setting, keyed to the phases of the Moon. Create a simple but meaningful ritual to observe at least the full and new moons, even if it's just spending a few moments in quiet meditation or journaling your thoughts and feelings. These regular touch points keep you connected to the lunar cycle and its influence on your personal energy and magical work.

Seasonal Altars

Dedicate a space in your home for an altar that you can change with the seasons and lunar phases. Decorate this altar with items that symbolize the current Sabbat or Esbat, such as leaves and acorns for Mabon or crystals and silver objects for full moon Esbats. This physical representation of the changing seasons and lunar cycle serves as a focal point for your celebrations and a constant reminder of the Earth's and Moon's rhythms.

Nature Immersion

Incorporate nature walks and outdoor meditations into your Sabbat and Esbat observances. Being in nature allows you to experience the energy of the season or lunar phase firsthand, deepening your connection to the natural world. Collect natural items for your altar or use these moments to perform simple rituals, such as planting seeds on Ostara or releasing something that no longer serves you into a body of water during a waning moon.

Reflective Practices

Use Sabbats and Esbats as times for reflection. Journaling is a potent tool, allowing you to record your thoughts, feelings, and experiences related to each observance. Over time, these entries will become a valuable record of your spiritual journey, showing your growth and the cyclical patterns in your life.

Crafting and Creativity

Embrace crafting and creativity as part of your observances. Make your own decorations, ritual tools, or talismans aligned with the energies of the Sabbats and Esbats. These creative acts not only enhance your celebrations but also imbue your practice with a personal touch.

Integrating Sabbats and Esbats into your solo practice doesn't require grand gestures or elaborate rituals. The most meaningful observances often come from simple acts performed with intention and heart. By creating personal traditions and regularly connecting with the cycles of the Earth and Moon, you weave a tapestry of spiritual practice that nurtures your growth, honors the natural world, and celebrates the magic within and all around you.

8

MEDITATION, VISUALIZATION, AND JOURNEY WORK

Meditation, visualization, and journey work stand as pillars within the realms of spiritual practice, offering pathways to deeper understanding, connection, and transformation. These practices, ancient in origin yet timeless in their applicability, serve as bridges between the conscious mind and the vast, often untapped, landscapes of the subconscious and the spiritual realms. Through meditation, practitioners learn to quiet the constant chatter of the mind, achieving states of profound peace and clarity. Visualization harnesses the power of the mind's eye to create vivid, sensory-rich experiences that can influence the physical, emotional, and energetic aspects of our being. Journey work, including astral projection and shamanic journeys, invites adventurers to explore beyond the physical constraints of time and space, venturing into other realms to gain wisdom, healing, and guidance.

These practices are not mere exercises in relaxation or fantasy but are transformative processes that facilitate personal growth, enhance psychic and magical abilities, and foster direct experiences of the divine or the universal energies that permeate all of existence. Whether undertaken for self-discovery, healing, communication with deities and spirits, or as a component of ritual and spellcraft, meditation, visualization, and journey work offer rich opportunities for spiritual exploration and development.

By understanding the techniques and principles that underlie effective meditation and visualization and by gaining an introduction to the intriguing practice of astral projection and journey work, readers will be equipped to embark on their own journeys of inner exploration. These practices hold the key to unlocking the doors of perception, revealing the interconnectedness of all things, and guiding individuals toward a deeper, more harmonious engagement with the world and themselves.

Techniques for Effective Meditation and Visualization

Meditation and visualization are foundational to deepening one's spiritual journey, enhancing mental clarity, and cultivating profound inner peace. These techniques not only support personal growth and healing but also strengthen the mind's ability to focus and create, making them indispensable tools in magical practices. Here, we explore methods to develop and enhance these skills, offering a pathway to more effective meditation and visualization.

Meditation Techniques

Finding Your Posture: Begin by finding a comfortable seated position that allows for a straight spine. This can be on a chair with feet flat on the ground or cross-legged on a cushion. A proper posture aids in deep breathing and helps maintain alertness throughout your practice.

Breath Focus: Concentrate on your breathing, noticing the sensation of air entering and leaving your body. This focus on the breath serves as an anchor, bringing your attention back whenever your mind wanders. Over time, this practice enhances your ability to maintain focus and stillness.

Guided Meditation: For those who struggle with quieting the mind, guided meditations can provide a structured path to relaxation and focus. These can involve journeying through a visualized scene or focusing on specific intentions or affirmations.

Mindfulness Meditation: Practice being fully present and observing thoughts, feelings, and sensations without judgment. This form of meditation increases self-awareness and helps develop a more profound sense of inner peace.

Visualization Techniques

Start with Simple Shapes: Begin your visualization practice with simple objects or shapes, such as a circle or a cube. Try to picture these as vividly as possible in your mind, including aspects like color, texture, and size. As your skill grows, move on to more complex images.

Engage All Senses: Effective visualization involves all senses. When picturing a scene or object in your mind, incorporate sounds, smells, textures, and tastes to make the experience as rich and detailed as possible. This multisensory approach deepens the impact of your visualization.

Use Memory and Imagination: Enhance your visualization skills by recalling a familiar place or object in great detail, using your memory to strengthen your mind's eye. Then, use your imagination to modify or create new, vivid scenes, practicing holding these images with clarity and stability.

Visualization in Spellwork: Apply your visualization skills in magical practices by vividly imagining your desired outcome as already manifested. Feel the emotions associated with achieving this goal, and hold the image and feelings as clearly as possible to direct your will and energy toward your intention.

Integration Techniques

Daily Practice: Like any skill, meditation and visualization require regular practice. Dedicate a specific time each day to these practices, starting with short sessions and gradually increasing their duration as you become more comfortable.

Journaling: After each session, jot down your experiences, challenges, and any insights gained. Journaling can provide clarity, track your progress, and reveal deeper understandings over time.

Combining Meditation and Visualization: Once comfortable with both practices separately, combine them to deepen your spiritual work. Begin with meditation to clear and focus your mind, then transition into visualization for specific intentions or explorations.

Meditation and visualization are powerful techniques that, when developed and applied with intention and consistency, can significantly enhance not only spiritual and magical practices but also everyday life. By cultivating a disciplined approach to these practices, you unlock new levels of consciousness, creativity, and personal power, laying the foundation for profound transformation and growth.

Introduction to Astral Projection and Journey Work

Astral projection and journey work represent some of the most profound and intriguing practices within the realm of spiritual exploration. These practices transcend the physical boundaries of existence, allowing the practitioner to explore other dimensions, realms, and states of consciousness. Astral projection, often understood as the conscious separation of the astral body from the physical body, enables individuals to traverse the astral plane, a dimension of reality vibrating at a higher frequency than our physical world. Journey work, encompassing a broader spectrum of spiritual travel, includes guided journeys, shamanic journeys, and other forms of consciousness exploration that may not necessarily involve separation from the physical form.

These practices have been described and revered in numerous spiritual traditions across the world, from ancient shamanism to contemporary metaphysical studies. They highlight a universal curiosity and inherent drive to understand the mysteries that lie beyond the tangible aspects of life. Engaging in astral projection and journey work opens up avenues for profound personal growth, healing, and the acquisition of knowledge, offering insights into the nature of reality, the self, and the interconnectedness of all existence.

Embarking on the Journey

For those drawn to these practices, the journey begins with cultivation—a deepening of one's meditation and visualization skills, as these are essential tools for navigating the non-physical realms. It also involves a thorough grounding in protective techniques to ensure the safety and integrity of the self during such explorations. The practitioner learns to set clear intentions, to call upon guides or protective entities, and to navigate experiences with both curiosity and caution.

The Multifaceted Nature of Astral Projection and Journey Work

Astral projection and journey work are not solely about exploration for curiosity's sake; they serve as pathways to profound spiritual insights, healing, and empowerment. Through these practices, one can encounter spiritual guides, access past life memories, receive direct spiritual teachings, and work through psychological and energetic blockages. These experiences, rich in symbolic and literal significance, often provide guidance and clarity regarding one's path in life, challenges, and purpose.

Navigating the Challenges

While the potential benefits are vast, it's essential to approach astral projection and journey work with respect and awareness of the challenges. Fear, doubt, and the possibility of encountering disorienting or challenging experiences require a foundation of spiritual maturity and psychological readiness. Practitioners must cultivate resilience, discernment, and a strong sense of spiritual protection.

Integrating the Experience

Equally important is the process of integrating the insights, healings, and experiences gained through astral projection and journey work into one's daily life. This integration is key to ensuring that the profound shifts and learnings translate into tangible growth, enhanced well-being, and a deeper, more harmonious connection with the universe.

This exploration into astral projection and journey work invites you on a journey beyond the ordinary limits of consciousness, offering tools, techniques, and considerations for safely navigating and benefiting from these extraordinary realms of existence. Whether you seek healing, knowledge, or a deeper connection with the divine, the journey within awaits promising revelations that have the power to transform not just your spiritual practice but your understanding of reality itself.

Using These Practices for Inner Exploration and Communication with Deities/Spirits

Meditation, visualization, and journey work are transformative practices that offer profound pathways for inner exploration and establishing deeper connections with deities and spirits. These practices unlock doors to the subconscious, allowing practitioners to traverse the landscapes of their inner worlds and engage with the spiritual realm in meaningful, communicative ways. Below, we delve into how these techniques facilitate personal discovery and spiritual dialogue.

Inner Exploration through Meditation and Visualization

Self-Discovery and Healing: Meditation and visualization serve as powerful tools for uncovering hidden aspects of the self, including shadow qualities, past traumas, and untapped potential. By directing focused attention inward, practitioners can confront and heal these aspects, fostering growth and integration.

- **Technique:** Use guided visualization to journey into your subconscious, visualizing a path that leads you deeper into your inner being. Encounter various symbols, landscapes, or figures that represent different facets of your psyche. Approach these discoveries with openness, seeking understanding and healing.

Accessing the Higher Self: These practices also enable communication with the higher self, the aspect of our being that remains connected to the divine source and possesses deep wisdom about our life path and purpose.

- **Technique:** In a meditative state, visualize ascending a staircase that leads to a sacred space where you can meet your higher self. Engage in dialogue, asking questions about your spiritual journey, life challenges, or decisions you face. Listen attentively to the guidance received.

Communication with Deities and Spirits

Establishing Connection: Meditation and journey work create the necessary energetic and mental space for reaching out to deities, ancestors, and spirit guides. Through visualization, practitioners can enter realms where these beings reside, facilitating direct communication and receiving guidance, blessings, and support.

- **Technique:** After grounding and protective preparations, use visualization to journey to a sacred space where you can safely meet and communicate with deities or spirits. This could be a temple, a natural sanctuary, or any space that feels safe and sacred. Offer respect and openness, inviting communication.

Receiving and Interpreting Messages: Communication with spiritual entities often occurs through symbols, emotions, and intuitive insights rather than direct verbal exchange. Developing the ability to interpret these subtle forms of communication enhances the depth and clarity of the spiritual dialogue.

- **Technique:** In your sacred space, ask your questions or share your intentions with the deity or spirit. Pay attention to the responses received, whether as images, feelings, or words. Trust your intuition to interpret these messages, and seek confirmation or clarification as needed.

Integration and Reflection

The insights, healing, and messages received through meditation, visualization, and journey work hold the potential for profound personal transformation. However, their actual value is realized through thoughtful integration into one's daily life and spiritual practice.

- **Journaling:** Keep a detailed journal of your experiences, reflections, and any messages or guidance received. Reviewing your journal can reveal patterns, confirm intuitions, and track your growth over time.
- **Creative Expression:** Translate your experiences and insights into innovative projects, such as art, poetry, or ritual crafts. This not only honors your spiritual journey but also solidifies the learnings and connections made.
- **Living the Insights:** Apply the guidance and insights received to your daily actions and decisions. Allow the wisdom of your inner explorations and spiritual communications to inform how you live, relate to others, and pursue your spiritual path.

Utilizing meditation, visualization, and journey work for inner exploration and communication with deities and spirits opens a rich, multifaceted dialogue between the practitioner and the unseen world. These practices offer a path to profound self-discovery, healing, and a deeper, more meaningful engagement with the divine forces that guide and shape our lives.

9

DEITIES AND SPIRITS IN SOLITARY PRACTICE

Embarking on a solitary spiritual practice offers a unique and personal journey into the realms of self-discovery, empowerment, and connection with the unseen world. Among the most enriching aspects of this journey is the development of relationships with deities, spirits, and ancestral guides. These relationships bridge the physical and spiritual realms, providing practitioners with wisdom, protection, and guidance. This chapter delves into the nuanced process of understanding, connecting with, and building personal relationships with these spiritual entities, highlighting the importance of respect, reciprocity, and personal growth within these interactions.

For many solitary practitioners, the call to work with specific deities or spirits comes from a place of intuition and deep inner knowing. Whether drawn to the gods and goddesses of ancient pantheons or seeking to honor the souls of the land and ancestors, the process of forming these connections is as varied as the practitioners themselves. It involves not only a journey outward into the rich tapestry of mythology, history, and the natural world but also a journey inward to the depths of one's soul and spiritual aspirations.

This exploration is not undertaken lightly. It requires openness to the mysteries of the universe, a willingness to listen, and a commitment to fostering relationships built on mutual respect and understanding. Through practices such as meditation, visualization, and journey work, practitioners can develop the skills necessary to communicate with and honor their chosen deities and spirits, integrating these spiritual relationships into their broader practice and daily life.

As we navigate the complexities of these connections, we are reminded of the rich diversity of the spiritual landscape and the boundless potential for growth and transformation. The following pages offer insights, techniques, and reflections for those seeking to deepen their connection with the divine, inviting readers to approach this work with curiosity, reverence, and an open heart.

Understanding and Connecting with Deities or Spirits

For solitary practitioners, the journey to understanding and connecting with deities or spirits is a personal and transformative process. It involves a blend of intuition, research, and practice aimed at establishing relationships that enrich and empower one's spiritual path. Whether you feel drawn to a particular pantheon or are seeking guidance from ancestral spirits or land spirits, here are steps and considerations to help you forge these sacred connections.

Exploration and Discovery

Research: Begin with research to explore various pantheons, traditions, and the nature of spirits relevant to your path. Books, scholarly articles, and credible online sources can offer insights into the historical worship, myths, and symbols associated with different deities or spirits.

Intuition: Pay attention to your intuition as you learn. You might feel a particular pull towards a deity or spirit—this can manifest as recurring dreams, synchronicities, or a robust and inexplicable interest in certain myths or symbols.

Cultural Sensitivity: Approach this exploration with respect for the cultures and traditions from which these deities and spirits originate. Understanding the cultural context is crucial, and it's essential to engage in practices that honor the integrity and sacredness of these spiritual entities.

First Connections

Sacred Space: Create a sacred space or altar where you can focus your intention and make offerings. This space serves as a physical representation of your desire to connect and communicate.

Offerings: Offerings are a traditional way to show respect and build rapport with deities or spirits. These can be as simple as lighting a candle, offering food or drink, or presenting natural objects like stones or flowers. The nature of the offering should correspond to the preferences of the deity or spirit, as understood from your research and intuition.

Meditation and Prayer: Regular meditation or prayer focused on the deity or spirit can help facilitate a connection. This might include chanting their names, visualizing their form, or speaking to them of your desire for guidance or support.

Rituals and Dedications: Simple rituals or dedicatory practices can further signify your commitment to building a relationship. This could involve crafting a dedicated ritual that aligns with the deity's or spirit's attributes or creating a piece of art or writing in their honor.

Fostering a Deeper Connection

Regular Engagement: Like any relationship, those with deities or spirits grow with regular engagement. Set aside time for rituals, offerings, and meditation focused on your deity or spirit.

Signs and Communication: Be open to signs or messages. These might come through nature, dreams, divination, or synchronicities in your daily life. Learning to interpret these signs requires patience and attentiveness.

Ethical Considerations: Always approach interactions with honesty and integrity. Remember, the goal is a reciprocal relationship in which respect and offerings are exchanged for guidance, protection, or assistance.

Journaling: Keep a spiritual journal documenting your experiences, feelings, and any signs or messages received. This can be a valuable tool for reflection and understanding as your relationship develops.

Connecting with deities or spirits is a dynamic and evolving process unique to each practitioner. It's a journey marked by curiosity, respect, and openness, offering profound insights and spiritual growth. By engaging sincerely and consistently, you invite enriching spiritual companionship and guidance into your solitary practice, deepening your connection to the divine.

Building Personal Relationships with Chosen Deities

Establishing a personal relationship with a chosen deity is a journey that unfolds uniquely for each practitioner. It's a path of mutual respect, dedication, and deep spiritual connection. Here are strategies to nurture and deepen your bond with your chosen deities, transforming your practice into a rich dialogue of divine companionship.

Developing Rapport

Consistent Offerings and Rituals: Regular offerings and rituals are fundamental in showing reverence and commitment to a deity. These can range from simple daily offerings of food, incense, or candles to more elaborate weekly or monthly rituals that celebrate aspects of the deity's mythology, attributes, or virtues. The key is consistency and the heartfelt intention behind your actions.

Creating Dedicated Spaces: A personal altar dedicated to your deity can serve as a focal point for your worship and communication. Adorn this space with symbols, images, statues, or items that are sacred to your deity, along with any offerings. This physical space strengthens your connection by providing a dedicated venue for your prayers, meditations, and rituals.

Learning and Living the Myths: Immersing yourself in the stories and myths associated with your deity can provide deeper insights into their nature and teachings. Beyond academic understanding, contemplate how these myths reflect in your life and spiritual practice. Emulate virtues, lessons, or attributes of your deity in your daily actions as a form of devotion and connection.

Communication and Guidance

Divination: Divination tools like tarot, runes, or pendulums can facilitate communication with your deity. Ask for guidance on specific issues and be open to interpreting the messages through the lens of your relationship with your deity.

Meditative Communication: Enter meditative states with the intention of connecting with your deity. Visualization techniques can be potent, allowing you to envision conversations or receive symbolic guidance in a shared sacred space.

Signs and Symbols: Be attentive to signs or symbols in your daily life that may represent communication from your deity. These can often be subtle and require an attuned awareness and understanding of your deity's domain or attributes to recognize and interpret.

Personalized Worship and Rituals

Crafting Personal Rituals: Based on your understanding and relationship with your deity, create personalized rituals that resonate with both their essence and your personal spirituality. This could include writing prayers or chants, composing music, making art, or performing acts of service aligned with your deity's values.

Festivals and Celebrations: Observe traditional festivals associated with your deity, but also consider creating personal observances that mark significant moments in your relationship, such as the anniversary of your dedication or significant insights or aid you've received from them.

Offering Your Skills: Dedicate your talents or skills as offerings to your deity. Whether it's crafting, writing, helping others, or any form of creative expression, doing so in honor of your deity can strengthen your bond.

Building a personal relationship with a deity is a dynamic process enriched by sincere effort, creativity, and the openness to grow and learn through divine interaction. It requires patience, as the depth of the connection can fluctuate and evolve over time, reflecting the ongoing dialogue between the human and the divine. As you continue to nurture this relationship, it becomes a cornerstone of your spiritual practice, offering guidance, strength, and a profound sense of belonging within the vast tapestry of existence.

Respecting and Honoring Ancestral Spirits and Guides

In many spiritual traditions, ancestral spirits and guides are revered and essential, serving as protectors, teachers, and sources of wisdom and strength. Connecting with and honoring these spirits can enrich your practice and provide insights into your heritage and personal path. Below are ways to respect and honor your ancestors and guides, fostering a relationship grounded in reverence and mutual benefit.

Understanding Ancestral Veneration

Cultural Foundations: Ancestral veneration is rooted in the belief that the spirits of the deceased continue to influence and protect the living. This practice is found across cultures, each with its own traditions for honoring those who have passed. Understanding the cultural context of your ancestors can provide valuable insights into how to approach them respectfully.

The Role of Ancestors: Ancestors can act as guardians, offering guidance and support. They are honored not only for their biological connection but also for the spiritual legacy they leave behind. Recognizing their continuing presence and role in your life is the first step in building a meaningful connection.

Connecting with Ancestors

Ancestor Altar: Creating an altar is a tangible way to honor your ancestors. Include photographs, heirlooms, or items that represent them. Offerings of food, drink, or items they cherished in life can also be placed here as a sign of respect and remembrance.

Offering Rituals: Regularly perform rituals that involve offering prayers, burning candles or incense, and presenting offerings to express gratitude and maintain a connection. These rituals can vary from simple daily acknowledgments to elaborate ceremonies on significant dates.

Genealogical Research: Delving into your family history can deepen your connection to your ancestors. Understanding their lives, challenges, and achievements can bring a personal dimension to your spiritual practice and veneration.

Working with Ancestors and Spirit Guides

Direct Communication: Meditation and journey work can facilitate direct communication with ancestral spirits and guides. Approach these sessions with respect, asking for guidance or insight and being open to the forms in which responses may come, such as feelings, words, images, or intuition.

Ethical Considerations: Always approach ancestral work with integrity, seeking a relationship based on mutual respect and benefit. Be mindful of cultural appropriateness, especially if engaging with practices from cultures different from your own.

Integration and Reciprocity: Honor your ancestors' guidance and support by integrating their wisdom into your life. Reciprocity is key; give back through offerings, live in a way that honors their legacy, or contribute to causes they care about.

Ancestral Healing

Part of honoring your ancestors involves recognizing and, where necessary, healing ancestral traumas and patterns. This healing work benefits you and clears negative energies that may affect your family line, both past and future.

Rituals for Healing: Create rituals aimed at healing ancestral wounds, asking for the support of good ancestors to guide and assist in this process. This can involve symbolic acts of release, forgiveness ceremonies, or offerings made with the intention of healing.

Continuing the Legacy: Part of healing and honoring your ancestors involves continuing their positive legacies. Identify strengths, virtues, and dreams within your lineage, and find ways to bring these into your own life and the world.

Respecting and honoring ancestral spirits and guides is a rewarding aspect of spiritual practice, offering a sense of connection, belonging, and support that spans generations. Through mindful engagement, reverence, and a commitment to healing, you can foster a relationship with your ancestors that enrich both your spiritual journey and your everyday life, bridging the past, present, and future in a continuum of shared wisdom and love.

10

HERBAL MAGIC AND POTION MAKING

Herbalism occupies a pivotal role in the practice of witchcraft, serving as a bridge between the practitioner and the natural world. This ancient art, rooted in the wisdom of the Earth, harnesses the unique energies and properties of plants to effect magical transformations, healings, and protections. At the heart of herbal witchcraft lies the understanding that every herb, flower, tree, and plant carries its own spirit. This essence can be collaborated with for a myriad of purposes.

The practice of herbalism within witchcraft spans cultures and millennia, drawing on a rich tapestry of knowledge passed down through generations. It encompasses not only the physical attributes of plants, such as their medicinal and nutritional properties, but also their vibrational energies, symbolic meanings, and mythological associations. This multifaceted approach allows practitioners to work with plants spiritually and holistically, blending science, magic, and intuition.

For the solitary witch, the study and application of herbal magic open up vast realms of possibility. Whether it's crafting a simple tea for relaxation, blending oils for ritual anointing, or gathering herbs under the moonlight for a spell of protection, the act of working with plants is both a ritual and a form of communion with the natural world. It's a practice that demands respect, patience, and a willingness to learn from the plants themselves.

Through understanding the basics of herbal magic, you'll learn to tap into the ancient wisdom of the Earth, creating potions, oils, and blends that weave together the threads of tradition, personal intuition, and the profound energies of plant allies. Welcome to the green path—a journey of growth, healing, and magical exploration.

Basics of Working with Herbs

Working with herbs in witchcraft involves more than just selecting plants for their magical properties; it's about forming a connection with the plant spirit, understanding the more profound energies at play, and integrating this knowledge into your practice. Here are foundational steps and considerations for effectively working with herbs in your magical and spiritual work.

Understanding Plant Energies

Each herb carries its own unique vibration and energy, influenced by its medicinal properties, growth conditions, and the folklore surrounding it. Sensing these energies requires tuning into the herb through meditation, holding it in your hands, or even spending time with the plant in its natural environment. This process helps to build a relationship with the plant spirit, facilitating a deeper understanding of how it can be worked with in magic.

Herbal Correspondences

Herbs are often associated with specific magical properties and correspondences, such as love, protection, healing, or prosperity. Familiarizing yourself with these correspondences can guide you in selecting the right herbs for your spells and rituals. Consider creating a personal herbal Grimoire or journal where you can record the properties, uses, and personal experiences with each herb you work with.

- **Love:** Rose petals, jasmine, apple
- **Protection:** Blackthorn, nettle, garlic
- **Healing:** Calendula, chamomile, lavender
- **Prosperity:** Basil, mint, cinnamon

Harvesting and Storing

The potency of an herb in magical work can be influenced by how and when it is harvested. Traditional beliefs often suggest harvesting herbs at specific times, such as at dawn or during certain moon phases, to maximize their energy. When harvesting, it's essential to approach the plant with respect, perhaps offering a small token of gratitude or asking permission to take part in the plant.

After harvesting, herbs should be carefully dried and stored to preserve their magical properties. Hanging herbs to dry in a dark, well-ventilated area is a standard method. Once dried, store them in labeled jars in a cool, dark place to maintain their potency.

Charging and Activating Herbs

Before using herbs in your magical work, it's beneficial to charge or activate them with your intention. This can be done through various methods, including:

- **Moonlight or Sunlight:** Exposing herbs to moonlight or sunlight can charge them with specific energies. Full moonlight is incredibly potent for charging herbs used in magical work.
- **Visualization:** Hold the herb and visualize your intention flowing into it, seeing it glow with energy that aligns with your purpose.
- **Elemental Forces:** Passing herbs through the smoke of incense (air), sprinkling them with water, burying them briefly in the Earth, or passing them through a candle flame (fire) can also charge them with elemental energies.

Practical Application

Incorporate herbs into your practice through various applications, such as creating herbal blends for incense, crafting magical oils and potions, adding them to baths for ritual purification, or using them as offerings in spellwork and rituals. Her versatility allows for creativity and personalization in how you choose to work with them.

Working with herbs in witchcraft opens a dialogue with the natural world, inviting a deeper connection with the Earth's cycles and the plant spirits that inhabit it. Through understanding, respecting, and aligning with the energies of herbs, you can enhance your magical practice, weaving together ancient wisdom and personal intuition in your journey of spiritual exploration and transformation.

Creating Magical Potions, Oils, and Blends

The art of crafting magical potions, oils, and blends is a traditional practice in witchcraft. It allows practitioners to harness the energies of herbs for specific intentions. These creations can serve a multitude of purposes, from healing and protection to love and prosperity. Here's how to delve into the alchemy of potion, oil, and blend-making, infusing your practice with the potent powers of plants.

Potions

Magical potions are liquid concoctions that imbue water, alcohol, or other solvents with the essence and energy of herbs. They can be drunk, used in baths, anointed on objects, or employed as ritual offerings.

Steps for Crafting Potions:

1. **Intention Setting:** Begin by clearly defining the purpose of your potion. This intention will guide your selection of herbs and the ritual process of crafting the potion.
2. **Herb Selection:** Choose herbs that align with your intention, considering their magical properties, correspondences, and synergies when combined.
3. **Preparation:** Cleanse and consecrate your herbs and workspace. You may choose to do this through smoke cleansing, visualization, or by casting a circle.
4. **Brewing:** Combine your herbs with your chosen solvent in a pot or cauldron. As it simmers, focus on infusing the brew with your intention, often chanting or visualizing the desired outcome.
5. **Straining and Storing:** Once the potion has cooled, strain out the herbs. Store the potion in a glass bottle, labeling it with its purpose and the date of creation. Some potions can be enhanced by charging under the moonlight.

Magical Oils

Magical oils involve infusing a carrier oil (such as olive, almond, or coconut oil) with herbs, creating a versatile tool for anointing, dressing candles, or as part of a ritual bath.

Steps for Creating Magical Oils:

1. **Intention and Selection:** As with potions, start with an intention. Select herbs and possibly essential oils that correspond to this purpose.
2. **Infusion:** There are several methods for infusing oils, including cold infusion (letting herbs sit in the oil for several weeks) or gentle heat infusion over a few hours. Focus and visualization during the infusion process imbue the oil with your magical intent.
3. **Straining and Bottling:** Once the infusion is complete, strain the herbs from the oil and transfer the oil to a clean, labeled bottle. Charging the finished oil under appropriate lunar phases can amplify its energy.

Herbal Blends

Herbal blends combine dried herbs for use in sachets, charm bags, incense, or loose-leaf tea, crafted to draw specific energies or support magical workings.

Steps for Making Herbal Blends:

1. **Purpose-Driven Blending:** Define the blend's purpose, which will guide your selection of herbs. Blends can be tailored for a wide range of intentions, from psychic vision to love attraction.
2. **Choosing and Mixing Herbs:** Select herbs that harmonize both in intention and aroma. In a clean bowl, mix herbs while focusing on your intention, charging each herb as you add it.

3. **Use and Storage:** Store your herbal blend in a sealed jar labeled with its purpose and date. Depending on its intended use, it might be employed immediately or saved for a specific ritual or magical work.

Creating magical potions, oils, and blends is a personal and creative aspect of witchcraft. It involves not only knowledge of herbal correspondences but also an intuitive sense of the energies at play. As you craft these magical aids, remember that your focus, intent, and connection with the plant spirits are as crucial to their efficacy as the physical ingredients used. Through practice, experimentation, and attunement to the natural world, you'll develop a unique alchemy that enriches your spiritual path and empowers your magical workings.

Ethical Foraging and Cultivating Your Own Herbs

Incorporating herbs into your magical practice connects you to the Earth and its cycles. Whether you're gathering wild herbs or cultivating your own mystical garden, approaching these activities with respect, sustainability, and ethics ensures that this connection remains harmonious and beneficial for both you and the natural world. Here's how to engage in ethical foraging and cultivate your own herbs in a way that honors the Earth and its abundant gifts.

Ethical Foraging

Foraging for herbs in the wild offers a profound way to connect with the land's spirit and energy. However, it's crucial to forage responsibly to ensure that plant populations remain healthy and vibrant for generations to come.

Foraging Guidelines:

- **Know What You're Picking:** Proper identification is crucial. Misidentifying plants can be harmful to you and detrimental to local ecosystems if the wrong species are disturbed.
- **Harvest Sustainably:** Only take what you need and never more than a small portion of any plant or population. Remember, you're sharing these resources with the local wildlife and other foragers.
- **Please respect Private Property and Protected Areas:** Always forage in areas where it's legally and ethically permissible. Avoid foraging in protected natural reserves or private land without permission.
- **Offer Thanks:** Recognize the gift you're receiving from the plant and the Earth. Many traditions offer a small token of gratitude or say a prayer of thanks, maintaining a reciprocal relationship with nature.

Cultivating Your Own Magical Garden

Growing your own herbs ensures a sustainable supply for your magical practice. It allows you to imbue your plants with personal energy and intention from the start.

Steps for Cultivating Magical Herbs:

- **Selecting Your Herbs:** Choose herbs that align with your magical intentions and are suitable for your growing conditions. Consider starting with easy-to-grow herbs like basil, mint, lavender, or rosemary.
- **Blessing the Seeds/Plants:** Before planting, you may wish to perform a small ritual to bless your seeds or plants, asking for the Earth's blessing and infusing them with your intentions.
- **Creating Sacred Space:** Whether it's a small container garden on a balcony or a dedicated plot of land, treat

your growing space as sacred. You might encircle the area with stones, create a ritual of planting, or place protective symbols around the garden.

- **Tending with Intention:** Water, weed, and care for your plants with mindfulness and love. Speak to your plants, share your energy with them, and listen to any messages they might have for you.

Sustainable Practices

- **Companion Planting:** Grow herbs that benefit each other together, either by deterring pests or enhancing growth, reducing the need for chemical interventions.
- **Organic Methods:** To keep your plants and the land healthy, use organic soil, compost, and natural pest control methods.
- **Seed Saving and Sharing:** Preserve biodiversity and strengthen your connection to your garden by saving seeds from your plants to use next year or to share with others.

Ethical foraging and cultivating your own herbs are practices steeped in respect for nature and its cycles. By approaching these activities with care, intention, and reverence, you not only enrich your magical practice but also contribute to the well-being of the Earth, fostering a deep and sustainable connection with the plant kingdom. This relationship built on mutual respect and understanding, becomes an integral part of your spiritual journey, grounding your practice in the rich soil of the Earth's abundant wisdom.

11

SHADOW WORK AND HEALING

Shadow work is an introspective journey that delves into the recesses of the self, exploring the hidden corners of our psyche that often remains unlit by the conscious mind. It's rooted in the understanding that within each of us lies a shadow self—a repository of repressed ideas, desires, instincts, and impulses that we've pushed away or ignored, deeming them unacceptable or incompatible with our perceived identity or societal norms. This concept, brought to light by Carl Jung, posits that actual personal growth and healing can only occur when we face and integrate these shadow aspects.

The process of shadow work is transformative. It challenges us to confront parts of ourselves that we may find uncomfortable or difficult to accept. Yet, it is through this confrontation that we find healing, acceptance, and a more profound sense of wholeness. Shadow work encourages us to ask why certain patterns recur in our lives, why specific triggers affect us so, and how we can grow from understanding these parts of ourselves.

Incorporating shadow work into one's spiritual practice, especially within the context of witchcraft, adds a layer of magical intention and ritual that can facilitate deeper insights and more profound transformations. Witchcraft, with its focus on the balance between light and dark, offers tools and frameworks for safely exploring the shadow self, aiding in the journey toward integration and empowerment.

Exploring the Concept of Shadow Work for Personal Healing

Shadow work is a transformative process that delves into the unexplored territories of the self, aiming to uncover and integrate the aspects of our personality that we have consciously or unconsciously rejected or suppressed. These shadow aspects often stem from our deepest wounds, fears, and societal conditioning and they can significantly influence our behaviors, relationships, and self-esteem. By engaging in shadow work, we embark on a path of deep healing, aiming to reconcile with these parts of ourselves to achieve a state of wholeness and authenticity.

Understanding the Shadow

The shadow self is a concept first introduced by Swiss psychiatrist Carl Jung, who described it as the unconscious aspect of the personality with which the conscious ego does not identify. According to Jung, the shadow can contain both positive and negative qualities that we deny in ourselves but can easily recognize in others. This can include traits such as anger, jealousy, greed, selfishness, or desires deemed inappropriate or unacceptable by societal standards.

The shadow also harbors potential gifts and talents that were suppressed due to fear, trauma, or disapproval. Shadow work helps to uncover these buried aspects, allowing for a richer and more nuanced understanding of oneself.

Benefits of Shadow Work

Engaging in shadow work offers profound benefits for personal growth and healing:

- **Increased Self-Awareness:** Shadow work forces us to look beyond the surface of our conscious mind, revealing the underlying motivations and fears that drive our actions. This heightened self-awareness allows for more authentic choices and responses.
- **Healing and Integration:** By acknowledging and accepting our shadow aspects, we can begin the process of healing old wounds and integrating these parts into our conscious life, leading to a sense of inner peace and wholeness.
- **Improved Relationships:** Understanding our shadow can help us recognize the projections we place on others, reducing misunderstandings and conflicts. It encourages empathy and compassion, both for ourselves and for those around us.
- **Unlocking Potential:** The shadow is not only a source of pain but also of untapped potential. Through shadow work, we can discover hidden strengths, talents, and passions, enriching our lives and our pursuits.

Approaches to Shadow Work

Shadow work can be approached through various practices, each offering a pathway to uncovering and integrating the shadow:

- **Mindfulness and Self-Reflection:** Regular practices of mindfulness and reflection help to observe one's thoughts and behaviors without judgment, identifying patterns that may point to shadow aspects.

- **Journaling:** Writing about your thoughts, dreams, and reactions can reveal hidden fears, desires, and beliefs, making it easier to confront and understand them.
- **Dialogue with the Shadow:** Visualization and meditation techniques can facilitate a 'conversation' with one's shadow self, allowing for direct engagement and understanding.
- **Therapy and Counseling:** Professional guidance can provide a safe and structured environment for shadow work, offering tools and support for navigating this complex process.

Shadow work is not a quick fix but a lifelong journey of exploration and acceptance. It requires courage, honesty, and patience, as the process can sometimes be uncomfortable or challenging. However, the rewards of this work are immeasurable, leading to a life lived with greater freedom, authenticity, and depth. By embracing our shadows, we learn to dance with the entirety of our being, transforming our darkest parts into sources of strength and wisdom.

Techniques and Rituals for Confronting and Integrating the Shadow Self

Confronting and integrating the shadow self is a profound journey of self-discovery and healing. This process allows us to embrace the full spectrum of our being, transforming hidden fears and repressed aspects into sources of strength. Here are techniques and rituals that can facilitate this powerful work.

Journaling for Shadow Work

Journaling is a potent tool for uncovering the shadow self. It provides a safe, private space to explore thoughts, emotions, and reactions that you might not fully understand or accept.

- **Daily Reflections:** Dedicate time each day to writing about your experiences, focusing on moments that triggered strong emotional reactions. Ask yourself what these reactions might reveal about your hidden fears or desires.
- **Dialogue with the Shadow:** Write a letter to your shadow self, expressing your willingness to understand and integrate its lessons. You can also write a response from the perspective of your shadow, allowing it to voice its fears, desires, and needs.

Meditation and Visualization

Meditation and visualization create a direct line of communication with the subconscious mind, making them practical for engaging with the shadow self.

- **Shadow Meet Meditation:** In a meditative state, visualize yourself entering a safe, sacred space where you can meet your shadow self. Imagine this meeting with compassion and openness, asking your shadow what it needs from you and listening to its messages.
- **Visualization of Integration:** Visualize a symbol that represents your shadow self (such as a dark figure or animal). Gradually merge this symbol with your own, visualizing a harmonious integration and acceptance of your shadow aspects.

Rituals of Release and Integration

Rituals can mark significant milestones in shadow work, helping to release repressed emotions and integrate shadow aspects.

- **Fire Release Ritual:** Write down the traits, fears, or memories you associate with your shadow on pieces of paper. In a safe outdoor space, burn these papers in a fireproof container, visualizing yourself releasing these aspects to transform and heal. Conclude by thanking your shadow for its lessons.
- **Cord-Cutting Ceremony:** This ritual can help sever the ties to past traumas or behaviors linked to the shadow self. Visualize a cord connecting you to these aspects. Using a ritual knife or your hand symbolically cut the cord, releasing its hold on you.

Affirmations for Shadow Work

Affirmations can reframe negative self-perceptions and foster acceptance and integration of the shadow self.

- **Crafting Shadow Affirmations:** Create affirmations that directly address the aspects of your shadow you're working to accept. For example, if dealing with feelings of jealousy, an affirmation might be, "I recognize my feelings of jealousy and transform them into motivation for my own growth."
- **Daily Recitation:** Recite your affirmations daily, ideally in front of a mirror, to reinforce self-acceptance and love.

Working with Deities and Spirits

Some practitioners find strength and guidance in working with deities or spirits associated with the underworld, transformation, or healing.

- **Altar for Transformation:** Create an altar dedicated to a deity or spirit that resonates with shadow work. Offerings, symbols, and prayers can facilitate a deeper connection and request their support in your journey.
- **Guided Journeywork:** Use guided meditations or drumming tracks to journey to the realms of your chosen deity or spirit, seeking insights and aid in your shadow work process.

Engaging in shadow work through these techniques and rituals invites profound transformation. It's a path that requires bravery, honesty, and a commitment to self-growth. As you uncover, confront, and integrate your shadow, you'll discover a more authentic, empowered version of yourself, capable of embracing life's full spectrum with grace and strength.

The Role of Witchcraft in Mental and Emotional Healing

Witchcraft, with its deep roots in natural magic, spirituality, and the understanding of energies, offers unique tools and perspectives for mental and emotional healing. This ancient practice provides a framework through which individuals can explore their inner landscapes, confront their shadows, and work towards a state of balance and wholeness. Here's how witchcraft can play a significant role in the journey of mental and emotional healing.

Empowerment through Ritual and Spellwork

Witchcraft empowers practitioners by giving them a sense of control over their environment and inner world. Rituals and spells are acts of will and intention that can be tailored to address specific areas of mental and emotional distress. For example, a spell to banish anxiety might involve casting a circle, burning herbs associated with calmness, and visualizing fears being released. Such practices allow individuals to externalize their struggles, engage with them through symbolism, and enact symbolic solutions, providing a sense of agency and relief.

Creating Sacred Spaces for Healing

The creation of sacred spaces is a fundamental aspect of witchcraft that can significantly aid in mental and emotional healing. Whether it's an altar, a garden, or a corner of a room, these spaces are sanctuaries for reflection, meditation, and connection with higher energies or deities. They offer a physical and spiritual environment where one can safely explore feelings, practice self-care rituals, or find peace away from the chaos of the external world.

Working with Deities and Spirits for Guidance and Support

Many practitioners find comfort and guidance in working with deities or spirits associated with healing, transformation, or protection. These entities can offer support, wisdom, and a sense of being understood and cared for on a spiritual level. Engaging with these beings through prayer, offerings, or meditative journeys can provide insights into the root causes of mental and emotional issues and suggest paths toward healing and growth.

Herbal Magic for Emotional Balance

Herbal magic is a cornerstone of witchcraft that leverages the healing properties of plants to support mental and emotional well-being. Herbs can be used in teas, baths, sachets, or incense to promote relaxation, reduce stress, or aid in sleep. By understanding the correspondences and energies of various plants, practitioners can craft herbal remedies that address their specific needs, grounding their healing work in the energies of the natural world.

Shadow Work for Integration and Wholeness

Witchcraft encourages the exploration of the shadow self as part of the journey towards wholeness. Techniques such as guided meditation, visualization, and reflective journaling—often incorporated into witchcraft practices—enable practitioners to confront and integrate their shadows. This work is crucial for mental and emotional healing, as it addresses the root of many psychological issues and facilitates personal transformation.

Community and Solitary Practice

While many witches work solo, the broader witchcraft community—whether online or in-person—can offer support, understanding, and shared experiences. For those dealing with mental and emotional challenges, finding a community that validates and encourages their healing journey can be incredibly affirming. Conversely, the solitary practice of witchcraft allows for deep personal introspection and customized healing rituals that cater precisely to an individual's needs.

Witchcraft provides a rich and multifaceted approach to mental and emotional healing, blending magical practices with psychological insights. Its emphasis on empowerment, connection with the natural and spiritual worlds, and the integration of the shadow self offers a holistic path toward healing and growth. By leveraging the tools and frameworks of witchcraft, practitioners can navigate their healing journeys with creativity, strength, and a deepened sense of spiritual connection.

12

LIVING AS A SOLITARY WITCH

Solitary witchcraft is a personal, transformative journey into the realm of magic and self-discovery. Unlike traditional coven-based practices, solitary witchcraft allows individuals to navigate their path, drawing from various traditions and practices that resonate most with their personal beliefs, experiences, and connections to the natural world. This path emphasizes autonomy, encouraging practitioners to cultivate their unique relationship with the elements, deities, spirits, and energies that permeate everything.

The solitary witch operates independently, crafting rituals, spells, and practices that align with their intuition and the rhythms of their life. This freedom enables a flexible, intimate approach to witchcraft, where personal growth, healing, and empowerment are paramount. It's a journey of exploration, where the witch learns from the whisperings of the Earth, the cycles of the moon, the lore of plants, and the depths of their inner being.

Choosing the solitary path doesn't mean isolation. Instead, it signifies a commitment to self-guided learning and development, where the practitioner becomes their teacher, student, and guide. It opens the door to creating a practice that is fluid, eclectic, and evolving, mirroring the witch's journey through life.

Integrating Witchcraft into Daily Life and Self-Care Routines

For the solitary witch, integrating witchcraft into daily life and self-care routines transforms ordinary moments into opportunities for magic, mindfulness, and empowerment. This seamless blend of the magical and the mundane enriches life with a sense of wonder and a deep connection to the natural world. Here are ways to incorporate witchcraft into your everyday activities and self-care practices.

Magic in the Mundane

- **Morning Rituals:** Start your day by grounding and centering yourself. Light a candle or incense corresponding to your intentions for the day. A simple sun salutation or a moment of gratitude facing the morning light can energize you and align your energies for the day ahead.
- **Cooking with Intention:** View cooking as a magical act. Charge your ingredients with specific intentions as you prepare them. Incorporate herbs with magical properties relevant to your needs, such as rosemary for protection or basil for prosperity.
- **Cleaning as Cleansing:** Turn cleaning your living space into a cleansing ritual. As you physically clean, visualize negative energies being swept away. Sprinkle salt water or sweep with a besom (witch's broom) to energetically cleanse your home.

Self-Care as a Sacred Act

- **Bath Rituals:** Transform your bath into a ritual for purification and relaxation. Add salts, herbs, or essential oils with properties aligned with your intention. Light candles, play soothing music and visualize the water washing away mental and emotional burdens.
- **Mindful Meditation:** Incorporate meditation into your daily routine to connect with your inner self and the divine. Use this time to reflect on your spiritual journey, set intentions, or be present.
- **Skincare with Intention:** View your skincare routine as a ritual of self-love and healing. Charge your creams or lotions with healing energy before applying them, focusing on loving and accepting every part of yourself.

Seasonal Living

- **Observing the Wheel of the Year:** Connect with the cycles of nature by celebrating the Sabbats and Esbats in ways that fit into your daily life. This can be as simple as a solitary walk to observe seasonal changes or as elaborate as a personal ritual to mark the occasion.
- **Gardening with the Seasons:** Cultivate a small garden or keep indoor plants that you tend to with magical intent. Work with the land, growing herbs and flowers that you can use in your magical practice and self-care routines.
- **Journaling Through the Seasons:** Keep a journal to record your observations of the changing seasons, your feelings, and insights related to these shifts. This

practice helps to deepen your connection to the natural world and your place within it.

Integrating witchcraft into daily life and self-care routines offers a profound way to live more consciously, connected to the rhythms of the Earth and your inner wisdom. By finding magic in the mundane and treating self-care as a sacred act, you create a life that is not only spiritually fulfilling but also nurturing on all levels. These practices serve as reminders that witchcraft is not just something you do—it's a way of being woven into the very fabric of your life.

Building a Witchcraft Practice That Evolves with You

Creating a witchcraft practice that grows and changes with you is crucial for maintaining a vibrant, fulfilling path that continuously meets your evolving spiritual needs. As you traverse different phases of life, your interests, challenges, and insights will shift, necessitating a practice that can adapt and reflect these transformations. Here's how to ensure your witchcraft practice remains dynamic and connected to your personal journey.

Continuous Learning and Exploration

The field of witchcraft is vast and varied, offering endless opportunities for learning and exploration. Embrace this journey with an open heart and mind.

- **Diversify Your Sources:** Expand your knowledge by exploring a wide range of topics related to witchcraft, including history, mythology, herbalism, divination, and different magical traditions. Books, online courses, workshops, and interactions with other practitioners can offer valuable insights.

- **Experiment with New Practices:** As you learn, experiment with new techniques, rituals, and spells. This hands-on approach will help you discover what resonates with you and what doesn't, allowing your practice to evolve naturally.
- **Reflect and Journal:** Regularly reflect on what you have learned and experienced. Journaling about your practices, spells, and rituals, as well as the outcomes and insights they yield, can provide clarity on how your path is evolving and which areas you're drawn to explore further.

Personal Rites of Passage

Marking significant life transitions with personalized rituals can deepen your connection to your practice and facilitate personal growth.

- **Craft Your Milestones:** Identify key transitions in your life, such as birthdays, anniversaries, achievements, or any moment of significant change. Consider what symbols, elements, or rituals best represent these milestones to you.
- **Create Meaningful Rituals:** Design rituals that honor these milestones, incorporating symbols, deities, elements, or practices that hold personal significance. These rituals can serve as powerful markers of growth and transformation on your path.

Adaptability in Practice

A flexible approach allows your witchcraft practice to shift and change in harmony with your life's evolving rhythms.

- **Listen to Your Intuition:** Your intuition is a powerful guide in adapting your practice. Pay attention to the shifts in your interests and energies, and allow these to inform the evolution of your rituals, spells, and daily practices.
- **Embrace Change:** Change is a constant in life and in witchcraft. Embrace it as an opportunity for growth rather than a challenge to your practice. Let go of practices that no longer serve you, making room for new rituals and approaches that resonate with your current path.
- **Integrate Life Experiences:** Use your personal experiences as a source of wisdom and strength in your practice. Challenges can be transformed into opportunities for shadow work, healing, and empowerment. At the same time, joyful experiences can inspire gratitude rituals and celebratory magic.

Building a witchcraft practice that evolves with you ensures that your path remains relevant, empowering, and reflective of your personal journey. It acknowledges that as you grow and change, so too will the ways in which you connect with the magical world around you. This approach not only fosters a dynamic and enriching practice but also cultivates a deep, enduring relationship with the craft that supports your growth at every stage of your journey.

Connecting with the Wider Witchcraft Community While Maintaining Solitary Practice

Solitary witchcraft is a personal and introspective path, yet connecting with the broader witchcraft community can enrich your practice with diverse perspectives, inspiration, and a sense of belonging. Engaging with fellow practitioners does not diminish the solitary nature of your journey but rather comple-ments it by providing support, knowledge, and opportunities for growth. Here's how to weave connections with the broader witchcraft community while honoring your solitary practice.

Virtual Communities

The digital age has made it easier than ever to connect with like-minded individuals across the globe. Online forums, social media platforms, and virtual meetups offer spaces where soli-tary witches can share experiences, seek advice, and learn from others without compromising their independence.

- **Join Online Forums and Groups:** Look for online communities that align with your interests and values. Depending on your comfort level, participation can range from reading posts and discussions to actively engaging in conversations.
- **Attend Virtual Workshops and Events:** Many organizations and practitioners host virtual workshops, rituals, and events that can be attended from the comfort of your home. These can be excellent opportunities to learn new skills and connect with others.

Occasional Group Rituals

Participating in public Sabbat celebrations, workshops, or open circles can offer a taste of group practice while you maintain your solitary path. These experiences allow you to observe different rituals and practices, drawing inspiration that can be woven into your personal practice.

- **Public Sabbat Celebrations:** Many pagan communities host public celebrations for Sabbats, which can be an excellent way to connect with the cycles of nature alongside others.

- **Workshops and Seminars:** Attending workshops on specific aspects of witchcraft, such as herbalism, divination, or spell crafting, can deepen your knowledge and introduce you to fellow practitioners.

Mentorship and Sharing Knowledge

Engaging in mentorship, either as a mentor or mentee, can be a fulfilling way to connect with the community. Sharing knowledge not only aids in your personal growth but also contributes to the collective wisdom of the witchcraft community.

- **Seeking a Mentor:** If you're looking to deepen your practice, seeking a mentor can provide guidance and support. Mentorship can occur informally through friendships or formally through structured programs.
- **Becoming a Mentor:** As you gain experience, consider offering guidance to those who are newer to the path. Sharing your journey can provide valuable insights to others and deepen your understanding of your own practice.

Respectful Engagement

When connecting with the broader community, it's essential to engage respectfully, recognizing the diversity within witchcraft practices. Listening to and learning from others' experiences while sharing your own can foster a mutually enriching exchange.

- **Embrace Diversity:** The witchcraft community is incredibly diverse, encompassing a wide range of traditions, beliefs, and practices. Approach interactions with openness and respect for this diversity.

- **Share and Learn:** While maintaining your solitary practice, sharing your experiences and learning from others can inspire and inform your journey. Approach these exchanges with humility and a genuine desire to grow.

Connecting with the broader witchcraft community enriches your solitary practice by exposing you to new ideas, practices, and perspectives. It offers support and inspiration while allowing you to contribute to the collective knowledge and strength of the community. By engaging thoughtfully and respectfully, you can forge meaningful connections that honor your path and the shared journey of all who walk the magical road.

BIBLIOGRAPHY

Black Tourmaline: Meanings, Powers and Crystal Properties. https://thefifthelementlife.com/black-tourmaline

Brain, J. L. (1982). Witchcraft and development. African Affairs, 81(324), 371-384.

Buckland, R. (2005). Buckland's Book of Saxon Witchcraft. Weiser Books.

Burning Sage. https://www.reneeshealing.com/post/burning-sage

Dark Feminine Energy: A Guide To Embracing Your Shadows. https://aestheticallychicbeauty.com/dark-feminine-energy/

Evans-Pritchard, E. E. (1935). Witchcraft. Africa, 8(4), 417-422.

Ghost Dreams | Dream Dictionary. https://www.dreamdictionary.org/meaning/ghost-dreams/

Higginbotham, Joyce & River (2002). Paganism : An Introduction To Earth-Centered Religions

Introduction to Magick: A Beginner's Guide - WECLUSTR. https://weclustr.com/introduction-to-magick-a-beginners-guide/

Know about tarot, and tarot cards! | Dream Infinity Brand 88. https://dreaminfinitybrand88.com/know-about-tarot-and-tarot-cards/

Manage Stress Naturally. https://www.thepointsofhealth.com/singlepost/manage-stress-naturally

Psychic Raina | Psychic Source. https://www.psychicsource.com/ourpsychic/raina-x3342?ac=vach

Sacred Sound Healing & Gong Bath | Son Boronat. https://www.hotelsonboronat.com/service-page/sacred-sound-healing-1

Solitary Witch https://witchcraftandwitches.com/types-of-witches/solitarywitch/

Surrender to Complete Healing | Thoth Readings. https://thothreadings.com/surrender-to-complete-healing/

The Enchanted Garden: Diving Deep into Herbalism's Role in Witchcraft. https://witchyspiritualstuff.com/the-enchanted-garden-diving-deep-intoherbalisms-role-in-witchcraft/

The Rede (An it Harm None) by Gaia Consort. https://gaiaconsort.com/track/2235950/the-rede-an-it-harm-none

What is ceremonial magic? – Authentic Spell Casters Reviews. https://verifiedspellcaster.com/what-is-ceremonial-magic/

What it Means to Be a Solitary Witch. https://www.mumblesandthings.com/blog/008

White, E. D. (2020). Solitary Pagans: Contemporary Witches, Wiccans and Others Who Practice Alone by Helen A. Berger. Nova Religio, 23(4), 146-147.

Wiccan Supplies: Setting up your Altar. https://artoftheroot.com/blogs/news/wiccan-supplies-setting-up-your-altar

Willis, D. (2017). Magic and witchcraft. A New Companion to Renaissance Drama, 170-181.

ABOUT THE AUTHOR

Monique Joiner Siedlak: Author, Witch, Warrior.

With storytelling infused with mysticism, modern paganism, and new age spirituality, Monique awakens your potential. Initiated into the craft at 20, her 80+ books explore the magick and mysteries of life.

A Long Island native, she now calls Southeast Poland home but remains a citizen of Mother Earth.

Beyond her pen, Monique craves new experiences and cherishes nature, advocating for animal welfare.

Join her captivating journey as she transports you to enchanting realms and empowers your own transformative path. Unleash the dormant magic within and embrace the extraordinary with Monique Joiner Siedlak's evocative words.

To find out more about Monique artistically, spiritually, and personally, feel free to visit her **official website.**

www.mojosiedlak.com

facebook.com/mojosiedlak

twitter.com/mojosiedlak

instagram.com/mojosiedlak

youtube.com/@MoniqueJoinerSiedlak_Author

tiktok.com/@mojosiedlak

bookbub.com/authors/monique-joiner-siedlak

pinterest.com/mojosiedlak

African Spirituality Beliefs and Practices

Hoodoo

Seven African Powers: The Orishas

Cooking for the Orishas

Lucumi: The Ways of Santeria

Voodoo of Louisiana

Haitian Vodou

Orishas of Trinidad

Connecting with your Ancestors

Blood Magick

The Orishas

Vodun: West Africa's Spiritual Life

Marie Laveau: Life of a Voodoo Queen

Candomblé: Dancing for the God

Umbanda

Exploring the Rich and Diverse World

Divination Magic for Beginners

Divination with Runes

Divination with Diloggún

Divination with Osteomancy

Divination with the Tarot

Divination with Stones

The Beginner's Guide to Inner Growth

Astral Projection for Beginners

Meditation for Beginners

Reiki for Beginners

Mastering Your Inner Potential

Creative Visualization

Manifesting With the Law of Attraction

Holistic Healing and Energy

Healing Animals with Reiki

Crystal Healing

Communicating with Your Spirit Guides

Empathic Understanding and Enlightenment

Being an Empath Today

Life on Fire

Healing Your Inner Child

Change Your Life

Raising Your Vibe

The Indie Author's Guides

The Indie Author's Guide to Fast Drafting Your Novel

Get a Handle on Life

Get a Handle on Stress

Time Bound

Get a Handle on Anxiety

Get a Handle on Depression

Get a Handle on Procrastination

The Holistic Yoga and Wellness Series

Yoga for Beginners

Yoga for Stress

Yoga for Back Pain

Yoga for Weight Loss

Yoga for Flexibility

Yoga for Advanced Beginners

Yoga for Fitness

Yoga for Runners

Yoga for Energy

Yoga for Your Sex Life

Yoga to Beat Depression and Anxiety

Yoga for Menstruation

Yoga to Detox Your Body

Yoga to Tone Your Body

The DIY Body Care Series

Creating Your Own Body Butter

Creating Your Own Body Scrub

Creating Your Own Body Spray

SUPPORT ME BY LEAVING A REVIEW!

goodreads

amazon

BookBub

Download on
Apple Books

GET IT ON
Google Play

nook
by Barnes & Noble

Rakuten
kobo